DATE DUE

			PRINTED IN U.S.A.

CRESTED KIMONO

CRESTED KIMONO

POWER AND LOVE IN THE
JAPANESE BUSINESS FAMILY

Matthews Masayuki Hamabata

Cornell University Press

ITHACA AND LONDON

First published 1990 by Cornell University Press.

International Standard Book Number 0-8014-2333-3
Library of Congress Catalog Card Number 89-46173

Printed in the United States of America

Librarians: Library of Congress cataloging information appears on the last page of the book.

⊗ The paper used in this publication meets the minimum requirements of the American National Standard for Permanence of Paper for Printed Library Materials Z39.48-1984.

FOR MY FAMILY

CONTENTS

ILLUSTRATIONS

PREFACE

This book is concerned with the lives of people I grew to know intimately in Japan, wealthy individuals whose families are engaged in private enterprise on regional, national, and international scales of operation. It documents the interplay of marital and filial relations in the attainment of power and the transmission of resources in a world in which families are also businesses. In this work, I have not attempted to untangle interlocking directorates or speculate about the degree to which owners versus managers determine the fate of family-founded enterprises. Rather, I have tried to learn how individuals make sense of their lives. Indeed, in a way that may seem extraordinary to some, this is a portrait of daily life.

The struggle with love and commitment, death and dying, self-fulfillment and self-sacrifice drew my attention and brought me close to individuals, whose search for meaning in adulthood revealed to me sources of human vulnerability and strength. Their fight for self-worth recreated, as often as it pitted them against, culture and society. Whatever actions they took, it became clear that their private dilemmas both shaped and were shaped by their institutional and cultural settings, especially those of the family. And in their life choices, the delicate relationship between person, institution, and culture became astonishingly clear.

While this book is about those among whom I lived, it is also about my own life, about my initiation into Japanese society as a Japanese-American. And so there is another kind of interplay at work, that of consciousnesses. It begins with an internal dialogue about my sense of life's commitments, which quickly extends to the Japanese engaged in this personal and scholarly narrative. By involving myself, my voice, I hope to bring the reader into the intimately negotiated reality of the field and the text. What is clearly heard and deeply felt in this ethnographic process is the dialogue between the consciousness of self and the consciousness of society. It is inescapably real, a compelling conversation for anyone who is struggling with the concerns of adulthood. It is that conversation that swept me, as I hope it will sweep the reader, into the currents of Japanese life.

Maxine Hong Kingston told me that it takes at least ten years to understand any human situation or enterprise. It will soon be ten years since I started writing, and I understand that this book belongs to many. To Maxine Hong Kingston, Ann Swidler, and Edwin McClellan for what they taught me about compassion, clarity and humanity. To Dorinne Kondo for the expansive spirit and scholarly insight that shape my work. To Jane Bachnik, whose criticisms give new meaning to the word "rigor." And, finally, to David Sneider, Scott McDonald, and Beverly Eliasoph, collaborators in personal, political, and intellectual escapades. I am also grateful to Holly Bailey and Marilyn Sale of Cornell University Press for their patient care and firm guidance.

M.M.H.

Haverford, Pennsylvania

CRESTED KIMONO

1 BOUNDARIES

Japan has always figured prominently in my life. At times it took on mythic proportions, especially when the elders of my family used our Japanese heritage as a weapon in our intergenerational and cross-cultural battles. In these struggles, we sought to define the language, and thereby the shape, of life's commitments.[1] With our metaphors at best mixed, we were, and still are, terribly confused about the meaning of self-fulfillment in the context of communal responsibility, of balancing personal desire with self-sacrifice.

Actually, the elders, especially those of the first generation, would never admit to being confused. Secure in their past experience with an ethical way of life in Japan, they played upon their grandchildren's personal and political insecurities, upon *our* vulnerabilities as members of a minority group in American society. Heated discussions would end when the first generation blustered, "Aren't you Japanese? How could you behave that way? You're acting like a white person." Our weak American voices failing us, we of the third generation would storm out. In the late seventies, however, it began to seem as though our grandparents were right. We were losing the argument. America was turning to Japan for lessons to be learned.

Scholars have presented Japan as a society in which an intricate net of obligations binds individuals together to make strong institutions of the family and, by extension, the workplace,[2] and as a society in which the traditional verticality of the family is successfully transferred to economic and political institutions.[3] Nurturance, warmth, reciprocal exchange, a sense of belonging also shape social life, in which the attainment of position does not mean the assumption of privilege so much as responsibility for others: in Japanese society a communitarian ideal exists at the very core.[4] These were the same idealized themes harped on by my grandparents, parents, aunts, and uncles—by anyone, it seemed, with authority and purview of my thoughts and behavior. Thus I was deeply distrustful of the accounts of Japanese society presented in the academy. Eventually, curiosity got the better of me, and in the fall of 1977, I went off to Japan to study the language and to see what the familial and academic fuss was about.

In Tokyo, my nextdoor neighbor was also an American student. Keith Robinson and I formed a close friendship as we tried to learn Japanese, not only in the classroom but also in the bars of the half-world of Shinjuku. We laughed along with our Japanese acquaintances as "Keith" was transformed into "Kissu" and "Matt" into "Matto." Keith's mother, worrying over his imminent starvation and, by extension, mine, kept us fed and in constant maternal contact from New York with a steady flow of Skippy peanut butter and Zabar's chopped chicken liver. Aside from being a skilled distributor of "care packages," Mrs. Robinson was the wife of a diplomat and frequently visited Tokyo with her husband, inviting us to the homes of Japanese, where we gorged ourselves on sushi and caviar.

The men and women who were our hosts were obviously wealthy. They were married, with children of my age, and with greatly extended families; they seemed perfectly composed, gracious, generous, and kind. Their circumstances were defined by family businesses, or *doozoku gaisha*; I found their gracious behavior in such a milieu impressive, for it seemed to me that *doozoku gaisha*, particularly those of large scale, were potentially explosive human environments, where financial and emotional investments become entangled, where the labor of love involves business as well as family, where sexual tensions can manifest themselves in material bickering and economic crises.

The situation seemed complicated to me, yet my hosts and hostesses seemed to have figured something out. They appeared to possess some secret about life and how to make it work. Thus, after a year of study, I left Japan with a highly developed taste for its cuisine, a sense of the language, and a feeling that I was on the verge of learning something important. I left determined to return as soon as possible.

Back in graduate school, from a distant perspective, I saw the *doozoku gaisha* as an ideal yet complicated unit of analysis. I saw the chance to compare various structures and processes of the *doozoku gaisha* so that I might gain a deeper understanding of the social order of the Japanese family and workplace. Through interviewing and participant observation, I hoped to understand the framework within which apparently disparate phenomena become an ordered whole for the Japanese. The central task, then, was to discover this framework.

I began with the assumption that the organizational aspects of institutions alone are inadequate for the establishment and maintenance of social order and for participation within that order. Scholars, such as S. N. Eisenstadt, have pointed out that those aspects do not guarantee: (1) that employees or kin would fulfill their obligations and perform their assigned tasks and roles, (2) that they would develop and maintain feelings of trust, (3) that they would implement collective goals, and (4) that there would be a feeling of commitment to the social order of the family and the workplace.[5] The construction of a symbolic universe is vital.

For Pierre Bordieu, the objective structures of the institutions of the workplace and the family are part and parcel of the creation of relatively permanent and structured cultural dispositions in the form of a symbolic scheme, which, in turn, structures actions in such a way that the objective structures of those institutions are reproduced.[6] For Eisenstadt, these "structured actions" are solutions to problems inherent in the potential arbitrariness of social interaction, solutions provided by the shaping of one's perception

3

of the environment by a particular symbolic scheme. In short, culture and tradition are important.

I returned to Japan in the fall of 1979 to look for "culture." And I found men and women, like men and women anywhere, trying to come to terms with how they lived their lives. As I became involved in their day-to-day concerns, the murky realm of culture took on greater clarity, and this clarity was a result of discovering analytically distinct planes of order within the *doozoku gaisha*: property, work organization, lineage, family, relationships between men and women, as well as the emotive and symbolic aspects of human life. Men and women of the *doozoku gaisha* devoted much time, attention, and concern to the processes of marriage and succession, and they revealed those processes to me with trust and intimacy. Marriage and succession, furthermore, meant the direct participation of people in one another's lives, involving them in such a way that activities occurring simultaneously on the various planes of order were brought together into a meaningful pattern.

Thus, a rich and complex sense of the world about me began to unfold, a sense of how men and women struggle to develop and maintain meaningful personal lives in spite of, and because of, the cultural and institutional contexts in which they live. But I am getting ahead of the story, for I must admit that I was able to identify and come to terms with that struggle only after fieldwork experiences forced me to engage in life and research in unexpected ways.

I started out by trying to interview presidents of manufacturing concerns, the heads of various *doozoku gaisha*. I was taken on a round of expensive dinners and luncheons: it was a polite and effective way of putting me off. Whenever I did get an hour or two for interviews, I would find the information on organizational behavior or structure within the respective firms to be of interest, but nothing new was being offered. Everything sounded much too familiar, and I began to wonder why I had traveled all the way to Tokyo only to hear what could be read in documents available at almost any American university.

When Mrs. Robinson heard that I was having some difficulty, she took it upon herself to apply pressure on her contacts in Japan, who happened to be the wives of presidents of various family businesses. They were part of an informal but tight social network. I became the responsibility of one woman in particular, who, while trying to get her husband to allow me entrée into the family's enterprise, brought me into her circle of friends. Mrs. Murata, who spoke to me only in English, would tell me at dinners or parties, "Don't worry. I'll get my husband to arrange a tour of one of our factories. Are you interested in research and development, too? I think my husband is organizing a tour in that division for several foreigners. Maybe he'll let you join them." Well, I did get to see a few industrial plants, but Mr. Murata seemed to be cooperating with great reluctance.

My association with Mrs. Murata, her family, and her friends created an opportunity to develop more contacts, as Mrs. Murata recruited others from her network of kin and acquaintances. A few of the women who came forward to help me were clearly feeling the weight of *giri* (obligations); I knew they were seeing me because of *giri* to Mrs. Murata for some past favor. Others came forward because they thought that by associating with me they would be able to enter Mrs. Murata's social circle, which reached into the Imperial Household. This second set of women were disdainfully regarded as *nari-agari* (nouveau riche and social climbers), but they turned out to be extremely helpful contacts; a few became my informants and, later, my friends.

Whatever their motives, women became saddled with the burden of my welfare and my research project. While they were trying to get their husbands to include me in their business lives, they began to include me in their own lives, first at public functions, then at more intimate gatherings. During those days and weeks, which for me were long and ridden with anxiety, the wives tried to cheer me up by entertaining me as a foreigner, and as our relationships developed, they began to tell me about their lives, about what they thought of marriage, about their hopes for their children, about love.

My first six months in the field, therefore, were occupied with trying to gain entry into the enterprise end of the *doozoku gaisha*. It was, to borrow from Clifford Geertz, my period of ghosthood.

As a nonperson, as a specter of sorts, I was often treated with deep suspicion in the guise of absolute indifference. A tremendous task, therefore, immediately confronted me: How was I to escape from ghosthood? How was I to create a totally new social identity for myself? For me, that process was hardly the elegant Geertzian experience, whereby one somehow crosses "some moral or metaphysical shadow line."[7] I became a person with an accompanying identity, with roles and obligations, by simply blundering about, by blundering across boundaries of culture, class, and sexuality.[8]

As a third-generation Japanese American, I had to negotiate the boundary of culture immediately: Was I inside or out? Well, the answer is quite simple: when I thought I was in, I was actually out, but when I acknowledged the fact that I was out, I was let in. Consider, for example, how a cabdriver in the city of Tokyo views the world. He (for it is almost always a he) is faced with a twelve-hour day, plying through the heavy traffic and often narrow streets. Life on the streets of Tokyo is, therefore, full of minor irritations, not the least of which is a fare who cannot give detailed instructions, for a written address means almost nothing in searching for the right house or apartment building. The ability to give detailed instructions is positively correlated with one's ability to speak Japanese; and since the cabdriver, like many other Japanese, may "adhere to an eminently biological definition of Japaneseness," as Dorinne Kondo put it, he may choose to avoid *gaijin* (foreigners), the outsiders.[9] On the distinction between "our people" and "outsiders" in Japanese society, Chie Nakane observed: "The consciousness of 'them' and 'us' is strengthened and aggravated to the point that extreme contrasts in human relations can develop in the same society, and anyone outside 'our' people ceases to be considered human. Ridiculous situations occur, such as that of the man who will shove a stranger out of the way to take an empty seat, but will then, no matter how tired he is, give up the seat to someone he knows."[10] This inside/outside dichotomy and the attitudes embedded within it are ideographically represented in the word *gaijin*, which is made up of characters for "outside" and "person."

The cabdriver, therefore, views the *gaijin* as clearly outside his own group, outside his culture, even to the point where a *gaijin* could not be expected to learn to speak Japanese adequately. This cultural construct of outside status is coupled with the reality of fourteen hundred years of racial homogeneity in the Japanese archipelago.[11] I, of course, entered the field phenotypically Japanese, and although the culture was not new to me in many ways, the language certainly was. After studying it intensively for three years, I was good at it, but not perfect. All of this meant that the cabdriver might happily pass by a *gaijin*, an outsider who couldn't be expected to give directions in Japanese, and stop for me, apparently an insider.

In one particular cab ride, I could pronounce the name of my destination perfectly, but I hadn't quite figured out how to say "right turn" and "left turn" in both the native Japanese manner and in the manner based on Chinese compounds.

> "Minami Aoyama onegai shimasu" (Please take me to Minami Aoyama).
>
> CABDRIVER: "Koosaten de usetsu daroo" (It's a right turn at the intersection, isn't it?).
>
> "Iie, migi e magatte kudasai" (Oh, *no*, please turn right).

At this point the car slowed almost to a crawl, and the cabdriver glared at me through his rearview mirror. He no doubt concluded that he had a well-dressed moron in his back seat. This incident was typical of my early experience in the field.

During the first few months of trying to gain entry into *doozoku gaisha*, I began to move slowly but surely out of ghosthood; nevertheless, I suffered in that liminal period between ghosthood and personhood. As someone with a Japanese face but an imperfect command of Japanese, I felt like, and was treated as, an incomplete human being. The Japanese were less than hospitable and often downright rude.

Many of the initial problems stemmed from my stubborn efforts to present myself as an insider, as a Japanese rather than as an American. I assumed that acting like an insider would accelerate

7

my integration into Japanese culture. I imagined that my Japanese face established a "familiar distance," often necessary for the gathering of information, even before I entered the field. In other words I thought that I would be familiar enough to the Japanese, so that they would feel free to speak about things that a "true" foreigner would not be expected to understand, and I also thought that as an American national, I would be distant enough to provide neutral space, in which the special frankness of ethnographic discourse could appear.[12]

I should have heeded Rosalie Wax's warning: "Perhaps the most egregious error that a fieldworker can commit is to assume that he can win the immediate regard of his hosts by telling them that he wants to 'become one of them' or by implying, by word or act, that the fact that they tolerate his presence means that he *is* one of them."[13] First of all, no matter how good one's Japanese might be, solecisms are inevitable. When one possesses a Japanese face, such mistakes are quite jarring to the Japanese listener, and so instead of being considered a rather talented foreigner who spent many years of hard work learning a difficult language, I was simply considered an undereducated Japanese at best and an incomplete Japanese at worst.

The trick for a Japanese American, I discovered, is to present oneself as an American—to shake hands and use English—when meeting people for the first time. The hospitable treatment normally accorded guests will then be forthcoming. Once having made one's entrée as a *gaijin*, however, it is possible to lose a bit of one's guest status as an outsider by switching into the Japanese mode. By switching, one is allowed to witness, and hear about, aspects of Japanese life that are often kept from foreigners because *gaijin* are considered incapable of comprehending particularly Japanese aspects of life. A sure sign of success is the following phrase, which precedes the most intimate revelation: "Yappari, nihonjin dakara, wakatte kureru deshoo?" (Well, of course, you are Japanese, and so you'll understand, won't you?).

In other words, one who wisely manipulates one's dual identity as a Japanese American could partake of the best of both worlds— the graciousness accorded to outsiders, as guests, and the intimacy reserved for insiders. If not, one is likely to experience the worst of both, that is, rude behavior and distance.[14]

By blundering about, I learned to manipulate my dual identity, but unfortunately I learned it at the expense of my original contacts. Through diplomatic circles, I had been introduced to members of one of the most elite of the large-scale family enterprises, one of international stature. Although they had tried to be kind to me during my first three or four months in the field, I confused them just as much as I was confused. Although I eventually learned to use my dual identity, I could not get rid of my early stigma of being an incomplete Japanese. As a result, the family members became increasingly polite and increasingly distant.

However, I had been seen with them at exclusive French restaurants and dinner parties in Tokyo, and so I somehow acquired some of their status. In the process of trying to pass me off to some other poor souls, my original contacts introduced me to more presidents of companies and their families. Much to my surprise, I became more and more a person in the eyes of this elite social circle. Suddenly, I was faced with the problem of crossing another boundary: class.

Now that I had become comfortable with my American and Japanese identities, I expected to be able to use my particular circumstances to enter into the lives of potential informants. By sharing some interesting tidbits about my life as a Japanese American, I hoped to be told about personal life experiences in return: a fair trade, I thought. Again, I was wrong, for my frankness about my background touched on an extremely sensitive issue in the lives of my growing circle of acquaintances and contacts. This circle was committed to the ideology that most Japanese are middle class, and they too would claim that they were middle class; yet they felt their lives were being encroached upon by ordinary people. One woman, for example, told me that she hated the arrival of festive days, for she would be forced to look at the tasteless silk kimono worn by ordinary women. The wearing of silk kimono should be reserved for women of good taste only, for women of position; yet this woman would claim, if asked, that she was *futsuu* (ordinary, average).[15]

I can still vividly recall the reactions I got when, in my naiveté, I mentioned that not only was I a third-generation Japanese American but that I was also of Okinawan descent (an ethnic, island people subjugated by the mainland Japanese during the Tokugawa and Meiji periods). The shoulders would drop as the back and neck straightened; the chin would drop, the lips pursed downward, and the following words would be spoken: "A soo desu ka?" (Oh, is that right?). Then a polite smile would appear as my partner in conversation disappeared into the cocktail party.

The meaning of this reaction became absolutely clear when one woman told me that she was delighted to hear that I was a graduate student at Harvard. She was proud of the fact that Japanese were gifted enough to enter the best universities of the world; however, she made it clear that this had not always been the case, for those who had emigrated to the United States three generations ago were the ignorant ones, the *heimin* (the plebian). This woman had assumed that my father was with a Japanese trading company in the United States and that I had recently emigrated. Her assumption: if one is at Harvard, one is of the upper class. How would I handle the fact that I wasn't?

Faced with a real fieldwork problem, with the fact of exclusivity, with the possibility of being shut out, I froze and offered very little information about myself. The tactic worked, and I learned an important code of behavior: *tatemae*. Japanese, unlike Americans, can easily accept duality in their lives; in other words, what appears on the surface may not necessarily correspond to the inner reality. Americans would tend to think that the inner reality is in some way "more real" and would, therefore, try to bring the inner to the surface. They would consider that to be honesty. Elite Japanese would see that as a sign of being ill-bred and ignorant, for the surface reality is just as real as the inner, private reality. The surface reality, the *tatemae*, exists for the smooth functioning of the surface world, the world of social relations, as opposed to the world of inner feelings.[16] As a general rule, one never looks beyond the *tatemae* in the social world. No one looked beyond my affiliation with Harvard University.

To *tatemae* one's circumstances often means to be passive, to simply accept others' assumptions about one's life. Unfortunately for me, total passivity was out of the question, for I was expected to act in the social world. This meant that I should have mastered a complex etiquette from degrees of bowing to degrees of politeness in language. The thought terrified me, for I knew that I would be exposed: no matter how strong the resistance is to looking beyond the *tatemae*, even the Japanese cannot resist a peek, if one forces the situation. And during my first six months of fieldwork, I gave them more than a peek.

For a while, *zabuton* (floor cushions usually made of polished cotton) were the bane of my existence. I first encountered them at a formal, very crowded reception. The *zabuton*, used for sitting on tatami (straw mat) floors, were lined side by side; and since I needed to get from one end of the room to the other, they proved to be somewhat of an obstacle. I handled the situation by tromping across them to the horrified stares of the other guests. Not only had I violated rules of etiquette, but I had also tromped across deep codes of purity and impurity.[17]

My instruction in proper behavior began with an informant showing me how to push my stockinged feet under the *zabuton* while *not* stepping on the silk-embroidered edges of the tatami in the balancing act of getting across the room. My lessons proceeded to the timing of the acceptance of a *zabuton*, the appropriate approach and movement toward sitting on one, and the conditions under which one should or should not hop off the *zabuton* to perform *tetsuki* (kneeled, floor bowing with hands placed directly in front of the body). These rules are: after the hostess leads one into the *kyakuma* (a room reserved for the entertainment of guests) and presents one with a *zabuton*, one should sit beside or behind the *zabuton* until she says, "Doozo oate kudasai" (Please be seated). Then one is to apologize by saying "Doomo sumimasen," before approaching the *zabuton* from the rear, placing two hands (with fingers curled under) on the cushion, moving knees forward, and finally sitting on the center of the cushion with legs folded under the body and big toes touching. When the host enters the room, one slides off the cushion to *tetsuki*: women place their hands in front of them so that they are almost touching and lower their heads to within three inches of the floor; men keep their hands about four or five inches apart and lower their heads to within five or six inches of the floor. When other guests enter the room, the *tetsuki* is not necessarily performed, for if they are standing, it may be rude to begin the process of *tetsuki*, thereby forcing them to the floor. It may, in fact, be more appropriate (and polite) to remain on the *zabuton* and bow informally: men should incline their heads slightly toward the floor with their hands placed on the knees; women should incline their heads but move their hands past the edge of the *zabuton*, placing just their fingertips on the floor, mindful that the little fingers should be kept ever so slightly afloat. As with any form of etiquette in Japan, the social context and the physical environment account for a high degree of precise variability in the rules. This made me feel as if I would never learn all of the proper forms of behavior. In fact, I had resigned myself to the real possibility of being closed out of upper-class social circles.

The rules, however, slowly became ingrained in my behavior, and they even seemed manageable in social situations that were purely Japanese. Multicultural situations, however, turned out to be impossible. One evening I attended a dinner hosted by a politician. Because of several European guests, the dinner was not the usual sex-segregated event. Wives were present and active participants in conversation. An elegant buffet was presented in the dining room, and dinner plates were brought into the living room for informal dining. It all seemed very comfortable, with a mix of French food and American manners.

Since I had deferred to the others, I was the last to go through the buffet line and the last to enter the living room. As I was about to seat myself, I realized that I was invading the social space of the guest of honor, the head of a Japanese household that once included a dramatic and powerful prince. In those split seconds, I executed a belated analysis of the seating pattern: the host and his male colleagues were lined below and to the left of a small sofa, on which the guest of honor sat and toward which I so presumptuously approached; a Japanese ambassador, the wife of the guest of honor, a European countess, the host's wife, and the daughter of a former South American ambassador to Japan were lined below and to the right. The politicians' wives were pushed into very crowded corners near the entrance of the room; they were farthest from the guest of honor. I had no time to change my course of action, and as I sat down, a look of resigned disbelief crossed everyone's face.

In those terrifying few seconds, I had belatedly drawn in my mind a figure of standard seating arrangements. Mr. Bun Nakajima of the Japan Travel Bureau provides us with an accurate, basic picture (Fig. 1).

The numbers in Figure 1 show the order of seating according to rank and/or status as a guest. The *kamiza* (places of honor) are directly in front of the *tokonoma*, which is the choicest area of the room and usually decorated with calligraphy or another treasured form of art. The *shimoza* (lower places) are at the farthest point away from the *tokonoma* and near the entrance.

By taking a place to the left of the guest of honor, I compounded my error by usurping his position as the highest-status male in the group. Again, I had blundered into another impossible situation because of my Japanese-American identity. While all the other foreign guests were assigned "guides," I was left to my own inadequate devices because I was thought to be essentially Japanese. At the same time, I was under the impression that the situation called for essentially American patterns of behavior.

Not knowing what to do with the elegant and clearly uncomfortable guest of honor, who was forced to share his loveseat with me, I blurted out in English: "I see you have a lot of watercress piled on your plate. I love the stuff myself." He smiled and said that he had acquired a taste for it while he was a student at the London School of Economics. The sigh of relief was almost audible. Another trick learned: use English in tight spots. This event proved to be a watershed of sorts, for it brought me right into elite social circles: the richer one is, the more social codes one can break,

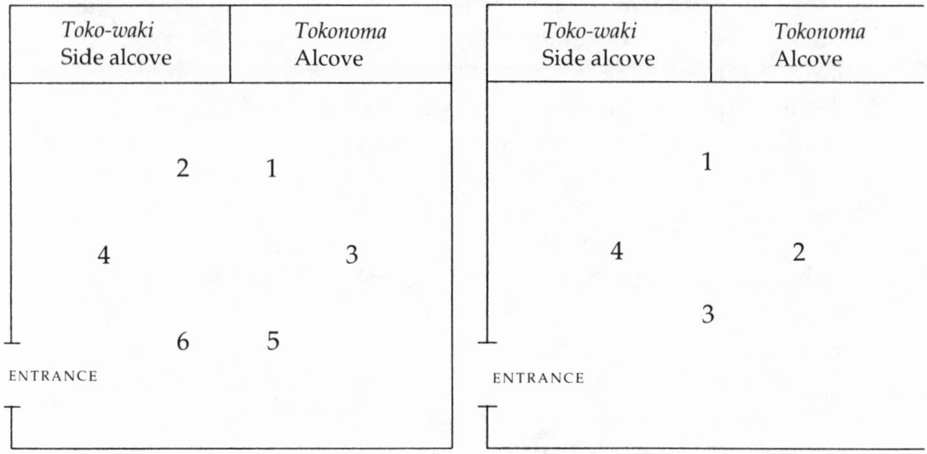

Toko-waki Side alcove	Tokonoma Alcove	Toko-waki Side alcove	Tokonoma Alcove
2 1		1	
4	3	4	2
			3
6 5			
ENTRANCE		ENTRANCE	

Figure 1. Standard seating arrangements. The drawings illustrate events with six or four participants. I have added the place of entrance, which was lacking in the original. Adapted from Bun Nakajima, *Japanese Etiquette* (Tokyo: Toppan Printing Company, 1957), 17.

especially if it is done with a bit of panache. And panache is often equated with having a Japanese face and speaking perfect English.

The boundaries of culture and class were to be expected. I was, however, taken by surprise when I ran into the boundary of sexuality. As an unmarried, adult male, I was considered to be sexually available and, therefore, a threat: young husbands were cool to me; daughters were nervous in my company; matrons circulated gossip about me. In the fifth month of fieldwork, my informants had begun to like and trust me, but because I was a sexually available male, it became more and more difficult for them to continue their relationships with me, and so one of them undertook to solve the problem.

Mitsuko Nishimura (née Itoo) invited me to join her for tea at four. When I arrived, she informed me that several of her friends

14

would soon drop by. At 4:10, a lecturer at Ochanomizu University came by; she excused herself at about 4:45. At 5:00, a graduate student in American history came by; she stayed until 5:30. The last guest, also female, was an intern at a university hospital.

"Weren't they nice?" said Mrs. Nishimura.

"Yes, they were."

"And they're all so intelligent."

"Yes, they seem to be."

"But these successful career women always have problems with marriage. It's too bad. They're all almost thirty, and if they don't get married soon, it will be even more difficult."

Panic struck. I retreated quickly, saying that I had a dinner engagement.

I thought that I had made a clean getaway from that informal *omiai* (the practice of arranging marriages). Mrs. Nishimura, how-ever, was not about to give up her chance to *endan o tsukuru* (make a marriage proposal), and so she called me the next day, suggesting that we lunch at the Imperial Hotel. I picked away at my chicken salad, as she tried to shame me into marriage.[18]

"Who are you to think that you could refuse to consider my friends? They're all from good families. Do you think that your family is better? Furthermore, any man of your age should be married. How embarrassing to think that you won't even consider marriage. Finally, you are being *fukoo*, undutiful to your parents." Her face wrinkled with annoyance.

The pressure was on, and in fact, I began to feel bad about my unmarried status. Overcome with cultural confusion, I began to babble on nervously in Japanese, apologizing: "Yes, I know that I should get married soon. Of course, a Japanese wife would be perfect. But I would make an inadequate husband given my cir-cumstances. I move about the world too much. My wife would suffer. My children would suffer. It would be a bad marriage. And so even my parents would suffer. I would be even more *fukoo* if I were to marry."

That convinced her. I won her over on her own terms. It was a question of what would be more unfilial: to marry or not to marry. I left the Imperial Hotel and wandered aimlessly about the Ginza, reeling from the prospect of being identified with the *fukoo mono* (unfilial child) among the Japanese elite. The boundary of sexuality appeared before me with great clarity. If I didn't cross it, I would waste my remaining months in the field, feeling dizzy with shame, my informants either trying to arrange marriages for me or trying to avoid me. As a sexually available male, I became my own biggest fieldwork problem.

From that point on, I acted increasingly naive about worldly matters. When my informants would ask me about the change in sexual mores among young Americans, for example, I would feign complete ignorance, or say, "Yes, I've heard about things like that, but really. . . . " My status as a student also came to the forefront; the image of the *gakusei-san* (student) is one of immaturity, even more than in the United States, and it is the image I cultivated. In Japan, patterns of behavior that separate the men from the boys are quite clear-cut, and I found myself adopting boyish language and tastes. I referred to myself only as *boku*, which is a form of the pronoun "I." A male could refer to himself in the more formal *watakushi* or the informal, extremely masculine *ore*, but I used the boyish *boku*. I, as *boku*, also developed a keen liking for Japanese sweets, French pastry, and Baskin-Robbins ice cream. Children love sweets in Japan, but boys at puberty learn to detest cakes and candies; and as men, they take to smoking cigarettes and drinking scotch.

The ploy may not have been entirely conscious, but it worked. By becoming a boy, I removed myself from the sexual market: no longer was I considered a threat. It was, at times, difficult to accept my identity as a sexually and socially immature male, and I still remember the shock I felt when one of my married female informants turned to me at a specialty food store in the Imperial Hotel Arcade and asked, "Boku wa nani ka hoshii?" By addressing me with the pronoun *boku* instead of my family name, she was assuming a very high degree of familiarity, indeed of intimacy. However, because of the age difference of about twenty years and her married status, it was an intimacy that was hierarchical in nature; in fact,

16

an *oneesan* (older sister) would address a younger brother with *boku*. My informant, therefore, was asking the Japanese equivalent of: "Does the little boy want something?"[19] It was, to say the least, irritating and embarrassing, but it was a mark of success: I seemed to have reversed the biological and social processes of maturing.[20]

One afternoon, early in my second year of fieldwork, I was in a taxi, giving directions to the driver for the quickest route to Roppongi, a major entertainment district in Tokyo. I was a bit worried about being late for an appointment with Mrs. Itoo, Mitsuko Nishimura's young aunt. My Japanese was perfect, if perhaps a bit too polite, but I apologized for its imperfection. The cabdriver was startled to find that I was born in the United States, and his curiosity was piqued. What was I doing in Japan? What number son was I? Was California rice really as good as Japanese rice? Along with my preferences in rice, he found out that I was still a *gakusei-san*, who was born the third son in a family of five siblings. At this point, he launched into a diatribe against the present generation of Japanese youth, simultaneously assuring me that the *mukoo no nihonjin* (Japanese "over there," abroad) maintained the traditions of Meiji Japan, and that I was an example of that culture, an example of a *shitsuke no ii* (well-disciplined) Japanese. He then told me that I was lucky to be a *san-nan* (third son), for I wouldn't have to think about marriage until long after graduating from college, and that I would benefit from being a *shachoo-no-musuko-san* (son of a company president) without being saddled with the responsibility of becoming the *atotori* (successor).

The cabdriver's comments confirmed that the creation of my new social identity, my *tatemae*, my Tokyo mask, had become complete.[21] As a *gakusei-san*, I was a socially immature male, not quite ready for marriage. As the number three son of an enterprise family, I was a fortunate, freewheeling, potentially irresponsible male of the monied elite. Furthermore, I was more Japanese than American; in fact, I was a Japanese of the old-fashioned, Meiji kind. After dropping me off at Roppongi Crossing, the taxi sped off, leaving me with thoughts about my Tokyo identity and the task of receiving yet another gift from Mitsuko Nishimura's aunt.

I had been caught up in a cycle of gift exchange with Mrs. Itoo since the very first day we met. In an early and gracious warning to me, Mitsuko said of her aunt, "She's much too generous." I had brought from the United States a number of Harvard University souvenirs: ashtrays, T-shirts, and the like. I had been forewarned that gift giving was a crucial aspect of social life in Japan and that I should be prepared. Those gifts, however, sat in their boxes for several months: that circumstance was, unfortunately, indicative of my life as a ghost. To become a person, one needs not only an identity but a role. My roles developed gradually through inter-action with others, and gift giving turned out to be a defining dimension of that interaction.

Gift giving in Japan is, to say the least, complex. The anthro-pologist Harumi Befu counted at least thirty-five different terms for gifts, ranging from "introductory goodwill gift" to "funerary gift."[22] A short list of the appropriate gifts for specific events and seasons appears in Table 1. A quick perusal of the list reveals how pathetically inadequate my Harvard souvenirs turned out to be.

In 1972 Befu collected data on the frequency and cost of gift giving among seventy-six Japanese households (see Table 2). In my early period of ghosthood, I exchanged gifts only three or four times a month. The initial outlay of about $100 at the Harvard Cooperative Society lasted for a little over three months. During my last eight months in the field, I exchanged gifts three or four times a week and easily spent from $100 to $250 a month on gifts.

The increasing frequency and monetary value of the gift ex-changes are measures of my increasing involvement in tightly knit groups as a person with more clearly defined roles. I must agree with Helmut Morsbach that keeping this involvement "going smoothly requires an acute awareness of reciprocal obligations and their appropriate fulfillment. These often function at the nonverbal level, and are mainly of a highly ritualized nature. Gift exchange is an excellent example."[23]

Gift exchange gives concrete meaning to three role-defining con-cepts in Japanese social relationships: *on, giri,* and *ninjoo.* An *on* relationship arises when one receives something from an *on* giver that one, as an *on* receiver, does not have. There is an expectation that this *on* will be repayed. However, since one cannot repay in kind (for one did not have the resource in the first place), the gift given in repayment is qualitatively different and noncomparable; therefore, in essence one can never repay *on*, no matter how hard one tries. As an *on* receiver, one is in a hierarchical relationship, in which one is the subordinate.

Giri, like *on*, is a concept based on social obligations; however, it is not necessarily one that is hierarchical. It can occur in relationships among equals, for example, between friends, neighbors, and classmates. A good person is *giri-gatai*, that is, someone who

TABLE 1
Appropriate gifts on customary occasions

Category of presents	Articles	Time of year
Otoshidama (New Year) presents	Postcards, white paper, *nori* (seasoned laver), cash	New Year season
Chuugen (midyear) presents	Luxuries, foodstuffs, articles of daily use	Beginning of July to July 15
Seibo (year-end) presents	Same as for Chuugen	About December 10 to about December 30
Presents for the Girls' Festival on March 3 and the Boys' Festival on May 5	Festival dolls	Middle of February to March 2 and middle of April to May 4
Shichi-go-san presents for children of 3, 5, and 7 years of age	Dresses, accessories, footwear	Beginning of November to November 15
Presents in congratulation of longevity	Woolen yarn, cushions, clothing of one's own making, cakes	The best time is the birthday of the person to be congratulated
Wedding gifts	Material for dress, accessories, sake, fresh fish, household art articles	Up to the wedding day
Presents in return for congratulatory presents given	Rice cooked in red beans, dried bonito, souvenirs, *furoshiki* (wrapping cloth)	No fixed date

19

TABLE 1—*continued*

Category of presents	Articles	Time of year
Offerings at a funeral service	Cash, wreath of artificial flowers, incense sticks for Buddhist services	The day before the funeral. Cash may be offered on the day, or sent later, if the donor lives far away
Offerings at a memorial service	Cash, molded cakes, flowers, fruit	Same day
Offerings at a Buddhist service performed during the equinoctial week	Confectionary, fruit	Same week
Offerings to a Shinto shrine or a Buddhist temple visited	Cash	Day of the visit
Remuneration to the priest at a Buddhist service	Cash	Same day
Presents given at the end of the mourning period in return for what is given in token of condolence	Tin of green tea, *furoshiki*	Thirty-fifth or forty-ninth day from the Buddhist funeral or fiftieth day from the Shinto funeral day
Presents in congratulations of the opening of a shop, store, or office	Wreath of flowers, sake	Opening day

Source: Adapted from Nakajima, *Japanese Etiquette*, pp. 78–79.

TABLE 2

Gift-giving events in 76 Japanese households

	Frequency per household	Total cost per household
Incoming gifts	13.2 per month	17,000 yen per month (about $57)
Outgoing gifts	10.2 per month	12,500 yen per month (about $24)

Source: Data first published in Morsbach, "Ritualized Gift Exchange," p. 100.
Note: Average period during which households kept records: 6.9 months (minimum + 1 month, maximum + 16 months). Total number of gift-giving events recorded: 12,600. Average value of a gift-giving event: 1,113 yen (about $3.70; exchange rates during summer 1972, when $1.00 equaled 333 yen).

recognizes and observes moral and ethical codes of conduct. "In short," wrote Befu, "*giri* is the normative force which attempts to maintain social institutions in a smooth-running condition, irrespective of how an individual might feel about the social order or about other persons with whom he might interact."[24] A gift given out of a sense of *giri* reflects and maintains obligatory relationships.

In sharp contrast to *giri* is the concept of *ninjoo*, the world of intimate feelings. Thus, a *ninjoo* gift is deeply personal. *Ninjoo* may, in fact, be in opposition to *giri*, to the social and the moral. This conflict is the stuff of tragedy. Befu observed:

> There is no satisfactory resolution of this dilemma. To honor the society's ethical codes requires suppression of one's feelings; but succumbing to *ninjoo* will cause social censure. Caught in this dilemma, there are three alternatives: one, to suppress one's private feelings and honor moral principles; two, to close one's eyes from moral obligations and follow the dictates of one's feelings; and three, to annihilate oneself through committing suicide, being able neither to ignore the society's moral obligations nor suppress one's personal desires. It is this third alternative which many Japanese have chosen and which has been dealt with in modern and traditional stories, attesting to the power of moral compulsion in Japanese society.[25]

At the other pole, of course, is the happy coming together of *ninjoo* with *giri* and/or *on*.

By embodying these ideal-typical forms of social relationships, gift giving shapes role expectations, and by exchanging gifts, individuals come to develop and modify their roles in relation to one another. Gift giving is a perfect example of the Geertzian concept of a cultural system serving as a model of and a model for social behavior; it both reflects and shapes human society. My first serious encounter with gift exchange involved Mrs. Itoo.

By February 1980, I had developed a close friendship with Mrs. Itoo and her only daughter, Sanae. We had been meeting frequently to discuss the prospect of an American college education for Sanae, and in fact, I had helped Sanae with her applications to Princeton, Columbia, Stanford, and other universities. By mid-February all of the applications had been completed, and the three of us gathered to celebrate and to talk about what college life in the United States would be like for Sanae. Mrs. Itoo's extravagant tastes dictated that we meet at one of the small but very expensive bistros that dot Roppongi.

Feeling a little lonely and lost in the city, I looked forward to outings with Sanae and her mother. Mrs. Itoo's penchant for dark capes and ropes of pearls and the sad ring in her laughter attracted attention and pleasant company wherever we went. Although Mitsuko Nishimura had alluded to family problems involving her aunt, Mrs. Itoo seemed to know how to enjoy life thoroughly.

This particular evening was not different from the others: interesting food and conversation. Just as we were about to part company, Mrs. Itoo handed me a small, carefully wrapped box and a card, saying that she was embarrassed at presenting me with something so inadequate in return for all the help I had given Sanae. "It's nothing," she claimed in English.

On the subway ride home, I discovered that I had received a Valentine's Day card and a box of chocolates. It was a small present, but I was touched. They had remembered that it was Valentine's Day, an event I had ignored in the United States but that, for some odd reason, had taken on significance now that I was separated from American rites and rituals. To say the least, I was pleased to find that Mrs. Itoo and Sanae had become my friends.

Delighted with my gift, I opened the box at home with the intention of sharing the chocolates with my roommate, and out fell 50,000 yen (then about $250) in five crisp, 10,000-yen bills. I was, at once, shocked, insulted, and hurt. "Who do the Itoos think they are? They can't buy me or my services!" My anger almost made me return the money that evening, but prudence directed me to make some phone calls first.

I called an American anthropologist, who called her informants for advice. I also called my Japanese informants. The Americans advised me to return the money, whereas the Japanese asked very specific questions: How did my relationship with the Itoos begin? What did I do for them? What did they do for me? What did I know about their financial status? How was the money presented? When was the presentation made? Did I want to continue the relationship with the Itoos? And so on.

My Japanese informants made the following calculations: (1)

since the Itoos had initiated the relationship and had acquired some resource from me that they did not possess, that is, knowledge about the American educational system, they were in an *on* relationship with me, and I was the *on* giver; therefore, the gift of money and chocolates was a return *on* gift; (2) because the gift was presented after I had completed my favor for them, it would definitely not be considered a bribe but a true gift of appreciation, a true gift of return *on*; (3) because of their circumstances, 50,000 yen was a small token, relatively speaking; (4) since the money was accompanied by a gift that was personally selected by the Itoos for an occasion that was particularly meaningful to me, it also embodied *ninjoo*, personal feelings; the *on*, therefore, was not mere obligation but was also backed with inner feelings; the gift was a combination *on/ninjoo* presentation; (5) finally, the gift was a sign that the Itoos needed me in some way, and if I were to discontinue the relationship because of that, I would not be operating in the Japanese mode, for the Japanese believe that one always has to depend on face-to-face relationships with specific individuals in order to survive in the world.

Given that interpretation, I could not have, in good conscience, returned the money, for it would have been taken as a slap in the face, and in fact, I had originally wanted to do just that: return an insult for an insult. With the help of Japanese informants, however, I came to the realization that the role that was developing for me in my relationship with the Itoos was that of *on* giver and that there was an expectation of magnanimity, of continuing that relationship of dependence. The gift, therefore, was an indication of a developing role and of developing role expectations.

I, however, did not feel as though I had made a real sacrifice by providing a bit of college counseling for Sanae, but I was afraid that my role as *on* giver would develop into something more than I could manage—that Sanae would finally attend an American university and I would be expected to be responsible for her welfare, in loco parentis. Given these realistic fears and concerns, I needed to modify the Itoos' role expectations, and this could be accomplished through a return gift.

What surprised me the most about making a return gift was the

23

exact monetary calculation made; that is, since a gift embodies ideal-typical relationships, a cost evaluation of the gift implies that there is a cost evaluation of the relationship. In fact, I was told that given my concerns, I should make a return gift that would leave me 25,000 yen ahead: the Itoos would then feel free to ask favors of me, to continue their dependence on me, yet I would be clearly setting limits on their expectations of me as an *on* giver. Morsbach pointed out that the "ideal value" of a gift is not divorced from its "monetary value" and that it would be "premature to conclude from this that the Japanese gift-giving customs must necessarily be devoid of feeling; it is simply that attempts at balancing obligations *exactly* are so much more important, and knowing the price of the gift allows one to do this."[26] In my case, it was not so much the balancing of obligations but the *modifying* of them that needed to be calculated *exactly*.

"When making a gift of flowers, you should go to Goto-san's place." That's the advice that I was given, and so in making my return gift, I went to Goto Florists in Roppongi and selected orchids, fifteen blossoms at 2,000 yen (then $10.00) apiece. I enclosed a note in English, saying that I truly enjoyed the Itoos' friendship but that they were much too kind. Our relationship continued long after I left Japan, but my role as *on* giver was delimited: sometimes I would get long-distance telephone calls from Sanae, who matriculated at an Ivy League university; she asked about course selections and the like; those calls were immediately followed by ones from Mrs. Itoo, who thanked me profusely, apologized for her daughter's selfishness, and asked me to dine with them again in Tokyo or New York.

After many anxious months, my new social identity began to emerge through a complex and delicate involvement with many patient and a few not-so-patient Japanese. As I began to discover that I had a few important resources that were not easily available to my informants, my role in their lives began to take the broad shape of *on* giver. I became an English-language tutor for the children, a college counselor, and a friend. As my social identity and my roles coalesced, I crossed the boundary between ghosthood and personhood.

Today, however, the person that I became in the field exists only as a shadow. I barely know him. And yet he overwhelms me whenever I return to Tokyo. He even dares to accompany my informants on their frequent visits to the United States, informants who now say to me, "Matto wa motto ii hito datta, ne?" (Matt used to be a better person, don't you think?). He inspires such commentary. In a sense, "Matto" judges me. He criticizes me for being too American, too selfish, too vulgar, for not being chaste enough. In fact, "Matto" has crossed a sacred ethnographic boundary by refusing to remain in the field, where he belongs.

2 PERSPECTIVES

After six months in the field, I reviewed my notes and was distressed by the data: interesting information on the business end of things, but nothing really new; interesting information on love and marriage, but its importance was unclear. Two events gave me new perspective and kept me from abandoning the research: the first was a cocktail party, and the second was a dinner with a president of a company and his wife at their home.

The cocktail party, in May 1980, was at the country home of one of Mrs. Murata's friends. Mr. and Mrs. Robinson, Keith, and I drove about two hours from Tokyo, and as our car, an old black Chrysler—a symbol of America's crumbling industrial base—pulled up behind the Cuban ambassador's silver-gray Mercedes-Benz at the entrance of the estate, I felt our arrival was distinctly shabby. Aside from the foreign ambassadors, there were presidents of banks, construction companies, and manufacturing concerns, as well as politicians among the one-hundred-odd guests. I was among the twenty or so "young people" at the party.

I learned at the party that Mrs. Murata, whose husband's firm was in electronics on an international scale, and Mrs. Itakura, whose husband's firm was also world renowned, were not just good friends but cousins. Their mothers were sisters. Through small talk, I also discovered that the young people's households

27

were in food products, pharmaceuticals, and finance. Furthermore, they were all related through their mothers; that is, their mothers and aunts were sisters. This was the first revelation: a kin network across industry through women.

The next revelation occurred at a private dinner several weeks later. It was, for me, another uneasy situation: in a suit and tie, I tried hard not to be an ungracious Japanese or a timid American, unsure of what mode of interpretation my behavior might inspire. Mrs. Okimoto, a friend of Mrs. Murata's, tried to get her husband to open up and talk to me, but at one point she was called away, and so I was left with the *shachoo* (president of the company), the servants, and dead silence.* I was relieved when the *okusama* (wife) returned to the dining room. She apologized profusely for being absent: she usually has someone screen her calls, but she had some urgent matter to discuss with her brother over the telephone. The awful silence at the dinner table was replaced by Mrs. Okimoto's energetic, effusive manner of speech.

By this time, I had become quite used to women's conversation, had developed the necessary vocabulary, and was, therefore, rather skilled at talking about family affairs. Mrs. Okimoto and I talked a bit about her older brother, her other siblings, and an upcoming social event, as the eyes of the *shachoo* began to glaze over with deep uninterest. It was, in fact, a social event that had made Mrs. Okimoto take the call from her older brother. Apparently, the Imperial Household Agency had requested that her husband's household entertain dignitaries at their country lodge. The preparations for it would cost approximately three hundred million yen for improvements that included bulletproofing; and the Okimotos would have to bear the cost for the honor of such a visit.

---

* In the process of reducing my social age because of the problem of being a sexually available male, I became, in essence, a *dependent*, low-status, as well as unmarried, male, whose case women had to plead. And in retrospect, it is small wonder that high-status males, heads of households, had little time for me. Cf. Michelle Zimbalist Rosaldo, "The Use and Abuse of Anthropology: Reflections on Feminism and Cross-Cultural Understanding," *Signs: Journal of Women in Culture and Society*, 5 (1980), 412–13; and Jane F. Collier and Michelle Z. Rosaldo, "Politics and Gender in Simple Societies," in *Sexual Meanings: The Cultural Construction of Gender and Sexuality*, ed. Sherry B. Ortner and Harriet Whitehead (Cambridge, 1981), pp. 281–301.

Since Mrs. Okimoto's older brother is the president of a bank, she asked him to expedite a loan for them. She explained to me that, compared to the United States, there is a high debt-to-equity ratio in Japan and that in fact her husband's firm is heavily indebted to a bank, of which her older brother is president.* At this point, the conversation ended with a sharp look from the *shachoo*. As I got to know Mr. and Mrs. Okimoto better, I found that Mr. Okimoto often accused his wife of talking too much about money. Fortunately, he did not make the accusation on this particular evening before I made an important observation, namely, of a woman actually using the network of kin across industry and finance.

Now, I found the two insights very curious; not only were women essential elements of the kin network across industry, but they were also, if Mrs. Okimoto was any indication, creating and using that network through their natal families. This was interesting because the Japanese household is structured, at least nominally, on a system of patrilineal descent. In the ideal-typical form of marriage, a bride is given away to her husband's household. She becomes a part of another household and is no longer part of her natal family. She is, in fact, treated with greater formality and distance by her natal family: in language and behavior, she becomes a guest in her family of birth.[1] The questions: What brings her back to her natal family? What makes her so involved in creating a network through her family of birth?

By asking these questions, my research perspective changed. The

---

* About the preference of family businesses for debt financing, W. Mark Fruin has written: "The predominance of family firms and their successful maintenance over many generations were related ... to the Japanese preference for debt rather than equity financing of their industrial ventures. Unlike the United States, where Wall Street and other large and well-managed securities markets appeared by the late nineteenth century, Japan's financial markets have attained stability and major status only in the recent postwar years. When firms sought outside funds in Japan before the war they often were forced to turn to banks for loans rather than to equity markets, with the result that firms, especially family firms, came to prefer loans to lessening control by selling shares. Accordingly, family control has not been as diluted in Japan as it has been in the United States by a steady reduction in the proportion of company shares that are closely held. Shares have commonly remained closely held in Japan, even if one or several banks have become influential at the level of the board of directors in family firms." *Kikkoman: Company, Clan, and Community* (Cambridge, 1983), p. 10. See also pp. 238–42.

29

importance of a submerged world that I had been dutifully observing and recording suddenly came to the forefront: the intimate
activities of the family, presented to me mostly from the point of
view of women, were no longer to be treated lightly. The problem
of understanding the reciprocal relationship between economic and
familial institutions, between work life and family life, took on
concrete meaning. With the change in perspective, the research
problem became: How might the *internal* structure and dynamics
of the household influence the realm of the economy?

Sociologists have usually drawn a neat boundary around the
family, isolating it from the rest of society for the purpose of de-
scription and analysis. The major approaches to the study of the
family fall to either side of that boundary: inside or out.[2] Both
structural functionalists and Marxists concern themselves with how
the family, as an institution, *reacts* to social forces; they look at the
family's external relationships, largely ignoring intrafamilial dynamics. Ethnomethodologists and social interactionists, on the
other hand, concentrate on observing the rules, roles, and relationships within the family by using sophisticated forms of content
analysis and by recording patterns of communication, including
body language. It is clear enough, however, that the internal dynamics of the family cannot be understood without the analysis of
the external and, of course, vice versa.[3]

By initially concentrating on the men of the household and on
business, I assumed several things: first, that the sphere of the
"public," that is, the economic and the political, took absolute
primacy over the "domestic," the familial;[4] second, that the direc-
tion of influence moved from the public to the domestic, from the
world of men to the world of women; and, finally, that the analytic
dichotomy between the public and the domestic existed in social
reality. My original perspective simply blurred my vision. Michelle
Zimbalist Rosaldo analyzed incisively:

> Our studies of domestic groups report their demographic flux and
> demonstrate how authority in public life can shape such things as
> residential choice and aspects of familial politics. But it remains the
> case that anthropological accounts, at least, have more to say about
> the organization of the public sphere (and so of male pursuits) than

of the real variations in domestic life because we think that social process works from "outside in." The contents of what we view as women's world is something all too readily conceptualized as shaped either by natural constraints or by the dynamics associated with men, their public dealings, and authority.[5]

From my new perspective on the women of the household, however, I looked beyond a unidirectional form of influence, beyond, as Sylvia Yanagisako wrote, "the recognition that domestic relationships are influenced by extradomestic, politico-jural considerations to the realization that domestic relationships are part and parcel of the political structure of a society."[6] The internal activities of the family are intimately related to the position of the family within the economy and the polity, and the way those two realms are organized is intimately related to the internal activities of the family, at least within the upper class in Japanese society.

Thus, as time passed in Tokyo, the analytic dichotomy between the public and the domestic began to collapse, and I came to understand, through experience, what both Yanagisako and Rosaldo had meant in their critical statements: the lives of men cannot be understood apart from the lives of women, and economic and political institutions, as well as familial institutions, are created by women, who act "as men's partners and/or competitors in an ongoing and constraining social process."[7] Family and enterprise were created and recreated as women interacted with other women, as well as with men, with those whom they saw at once as allies and competitors, with those whom they at once loved and despised.

3 HOUSEHOLDS

The embrace of interdependence, secure and sometimes bitter, may seem inescapably natural to men and women who choose to immerse themselves in marriage and child rearing. In the minor day-to-day crises that call for decisions that are immediate, almost instinctive, the structure of life is reproduced with an almost unerring sense of ethics, grounded in the reproduction of "natural" patterns of human behavior, seemingly without variation from the past or across cultures. The patterns thus seem to lie beyond the realm of the socially constructed. Relationships between men and women, sexual, emotional, and material, are most susceptible to this feeling of the natural. However, it was the sociological reality of the household in Japan as a design for living, rather than its biogenetic morphology, that informed the life choices of those I came to know in Tokyo.

In terms of traditional ideals, the *ie* is patriarchal, patrilineal, primogenitural, and patrilocal. Succession to the headship of the household is reserved, ideally, for the eldest son, who inherits the household property as part of the process of succession. The eldest son also inherits the responsibility of caring for his aged parents, with whom he resides. Younger sons establish branch families with the aid of the main family. Financial aid given to younger sons to support their efforts at branching is likened to the dowries that daughters take with them when they marry out: both are forms of

33

premortem inheritance. A marriage, preferably arranged, has more to do with the interests of the *ie* as a whole than with those of the man and woman as individuals. In terms of intrahousehold status, the system calls for a ranking of the aged over the young, elder sons over younger, sons over daughters, males over females.

In actual practice, however, much of this ideal is routinely ignored. For example, the position of household head is preferentially reserved for the eldest son; if, however, he seems to lack the adequate skills or temperament to assume the role, he is passed over, and the position is made available to a younger son, or to a *muko-yooshi*, an adopted son brought into the *ie* through marriage with a daughter. If there are no children in the family, a girl might be brought in for fosterage, then married, and her husband brought in through adoption; or both a husband and a wife might be brought in as *fufu-yooshi*, a married pair brought into the *ie* through adoption. If a wife is widowed, she may assume temporary headship of the household until her son reaches maturity. In other words, there are any number of strategies, although some are preferred over others, for filling the position of household head, *just as long as the position is filled.*

Indeed, the *ie* looks less like a family and more like a corporate group with a variety of options available to it to fill positions and thereby guarantee organizational survival.[1] John C. Pelzel made it very clear that the concept of lineage in Japan is not primarily used to render genetic relationships understandable, for "many genetically related households may not so associate themselves, and extant households may be . . . replaced by units bound only by ties of fictitious kinship." Pelzel suggested that the concept of lineage is used, instead, to understand and to organize power and mobilize resources. Thus, it is the socioeconomic reality of the *ie*, rather than its biogenetic morphology, that makes it available as a template for realms of social life other than the familial.[2]

Hironobu Kitaoji takes this point one step further in his study of the Japanese household. Kitaoji maintains that the *ie* is a perpetual social organization, like a corporation. This is most clearly seen in recruitment. Any organization is faced with the problem of recruiting members with the passing of time, with the turnover

TABLE 3
Three types of positional succession

	Means of recruitment to position of househead	Means of recruitment to position of housewife	Conventional practice
Type 1	Consanguinity or fosterage	Adoption	Virilocal marriage
Type 2	Adoption	Consanguinity or fosterage	Uxorilocal marriage or adoptive marriage
Type 3	Adoption	Adoption	Adoption of a married couple

Source: Adapted from Kitaoji, "Structure of the Japanese Family," p. 1048. The term *adoption* is used here in the sense of acquisition of permanent membership in a family by an adult. The terms *consanguinity* and *fosterage* mean the acquisition of permanent membership in a family at birth and in childhood, respectively.

in generations. The Japanese household's solution to that problem, unlike the nuclear family's or the extended family's solutions, does not depend on rules of descent or rules of postmarital residence. In other words, it does not depend on birth, nor does it depend on physical/geographic location. Instead, the *ie*'s solution entails more abstract structural/organizational concepts of succession and inheritance. Thus, the rules of succession and inheritance determine the nature of generational change in the Japanese family.

Kitaoji outlines four rules of succession and inheritance:

Rule 1. Physical kinship is preferred to social kinship.
Rule 2. The succession of householdship has priority over that of housewifeship.
Rule 3. Rule 1 has priority over rule 2 in the case of inheritance.
Rule 4. It is possible to skip one generation in the transmission of family property.[3]

These rules operate in three types of succession (Table 3). According to the four rules of succession and inheritance, the type 1 form of succession in Table 3 is preferred over types 2 and 3, for only in type 1 is the successor to the headship recruited through consanguinity or fosterage. In type 1, the son or foster son marries-in a woman, who then, as an *oyome-san* (bride), becomes part of his household. Type 2 is preferred over type 3, for it ensures physical

35

kinship between the incumbent household head and household wife and the succeeding generation. In the type 2 case, a daughter marries-in a *muko-yooshi* (male bride), that is, a man who gives up claims on his natal family and is adopted into his wife's household.

Rule 3 means that the successor to househeadship in types 1 and 3 would inherit the family property. In type 2, the successor to the household wifeship, the woman who brings in the *muko-yooshi*, is the inheritor of family property. Because of rule 4, however, it is possible that neither the successor to the household headship nor the household wifeship in types 2 and 3 will inherit the family property; instead, they act as "regents," who manage the property that is legally transferred to one of their children or to one that is brought in through the many strategies of adoption.

The *ie* is not locked into the biogenetic reality of birth, descent, and lineage. Its social organizational and structural principles operate in stark contrast to its ideology of biology, of patrilineal descent and primogeniture. The tragic story, therefore, of the spoiled *choonan* (eldest son) who is pushed aside to make way for his sister's *muko-yooshi* (rather, his *household's* male bride) for reasons of superior talent and/or political/economic alliances is grounded in the facts of organizational behavior within the *ie*.

A comparison of Figures 2, 3, and 4, which illustrate the developmental cycles of the nuclear family, the *ie*, and the extended family, highlights the *ie* as an organization that operates on structural principles. Positions within the organization are not only filled but reproduced over time in its *original form*: individuals may come and go, but the organization continues in perpetuity.

The nuclear family is ephemeral because its continued existence as an organization is highly dependent on the life cycle or behavior of individuals. The existence of the original nuclear family N in Figure 2 is determined by individual members, for it lasts only until the death of the original $n-1$ and $n-2$ and the marriage of their children $n-3$ and $n-4$. With the generational change, the death of father $n-1$ and mother $n-2$, only sister $n-4$ is left in the original family N. Brother $n-3$ has already married and has created a *new* family N'. If sister $n-4$ should die or marry, then the original family

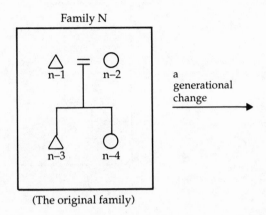

Family N

a
generational
change

(The original family)

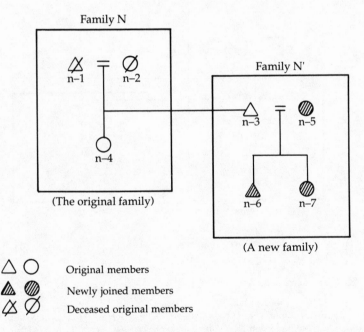

Family N

(The original family)

Family N'

(A new family)

△ ○ Original members
△ ◎ Newly joined members
△ ∅ Deceased original members

Figure 2. **The developmental cycle of the nuclear family. Adapted from Hironobu Kitaoji, "The Structure of the Japanese Family,"** *American Anthropologist,* **73 (1971), 1051.**

37

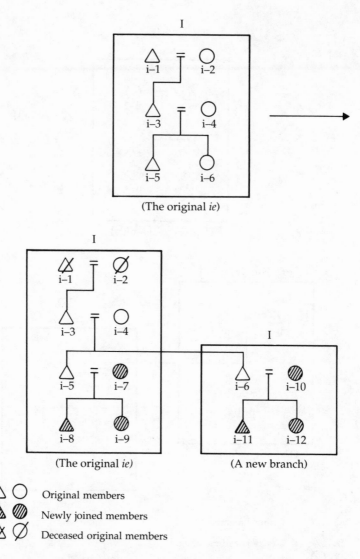

Original members

Newly joined members

Deceased original members

Figure 3. The developmental cycle of the *ie*. Adapted from Hironobu Kitaoji, "The Structure of the Japanese Family," *American Anthropologist*, 73 (1971), 1052. The drawing was originally called "The Developmental Cycle of the Stem Family." I gave it its new title for the sake of clarity and consistency. Thus, "i–1," for example, was "s–1" in the original.

Family E

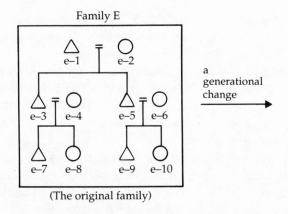

a
generational
change

→

(The original family)

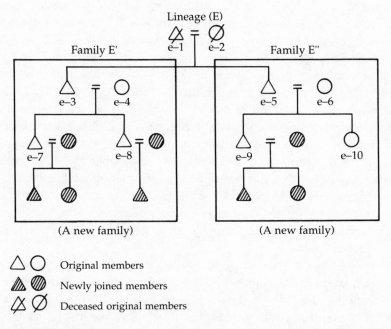

Lineage (E)

Family E'   Family E"

(A new family)   (A new family)

△ ○   Original members
▲ ◉   Newly joined members
◿ ⊘   Deceased original members

Figure 4. The developmental cycle of the extended family. Adapted from Hironobu Kitaoji, "The Structure of the Japanese Family," *American Anthropologist*, 73 (1971), 1053. I have added "e–3," "e–4," "e–5," "e–6," "e–7," "e–8," "e–9," and "e–10" to "Lineage (E)," which were lacking in the original.

N will have completely disappeared. Because individuals make up the positions, the nuclear family is, in essence, transitory.

After generational change, the original *ie I* in Figure 3 is not modified in basic organizational structure. After the househead *i–*1 and his wife *i–*2 die, their son *i–*3 and their daughter-in-law *i–*4 assume their positions; or their daughter and their adopted son-in-law (the *muko-yooshi*) will assume their positions, and this continues on with their grandson *i–*5 and his wife *i–*7. Because no other married siblings may stay in the original family *I*, the number of permanent positions within the household remains the same: that is, two, the household headship and the household wifeship. Since the filling of the positions does not depend on biological descent, the original *I* continues in perpetuity in its basic organizational form, completely independent of individual participation. It is, indeed, a perpetual social organization.

The extended family, like the nuclear family, is ephemeral but in a completely different way. In Figure 4, after the death of father *e–*1 and mother *e–*2 in the original extended family *E*, two *new* families are created out of *e–*3 = *e–*4 and *e–*5 = *e–*6. The original extended family *E* has completely disappeared and has been transformed into Lineage (*E*). The line of descent exists, but the original family has disappeared. Furthermore, since siblings live together after marriage, the number of permanent positions in an original extended family is expandable. Here, the group accommodates individuals, whereas, in the Japanese household, the number of permanent positions is firmly limited: individuals accommodate the organization.

The *ie*, therefore, is a perfect example of sociocentric forms of organizational life. Simply because it is not made up of individuals but of positions, the *ie's* existence, unlike that of the nuclear family's or the extended family's, is highly resistant to the unpredictability of individual characteristics and behavior. As Bachnik pointed out:

> Positional organization means that *ie* succession is not contingent on the maintenance of any specific form for the organization of its successors, and thus allows the widest possibilities for succession options; that the organization should continue takes precedence over how it continues. Positions thus provide flexibility for ensuring

succession in the *ie*, because they allow it to be organized pragmatically. "Position" allows the continuity of the *ie* to be removed (one step) from the disposition of the human successors. They may become ill or mismanage their duties. Positions, not personal relationships, also provide the "formal" regularity of the *ie*.[4]

What more could be asked of an organization? It is for this reason that the *ie* has served and continues to serve as a template for institutions other than the family in Japanese society.[5]

The fact that the Japanese *ie* is made up of positions rather than individuals took on real meaning for me as I witnessed household heads and *okusama* discuss the future of their *ie*. In early 1980, a professional matchmaker, dressed in a kimono and smelling of camphor, appeared at the doorstep of the Okimotos' main family, much to everyone's surprise. A wily old man, he needed no introduction at the Okimotos', for he had arranged the marriage of Mr. and Mrs. Okimoto. He was especially familiar to Mrs. Okimoto, since he had handled many of the marriages of her natal family, whose businesses had been nearly dismantled with the postwar reforms toward democratization. In fact, Mrs. Okimoto felt *on*, an unrepayable social debt, toward him. She believed that it was partially through his efforts at arranging good marriages that her natal family had been able to make a suitable recovery from the devastation of the war.

The Okimotos' eldest daughter, the *choojo*, had just turned twenty and was, therefore, in the early stages of being *tekireiki* (in one's prime time for marriage).[6] The matchmaker kept elaborate records of "his" households and had known about the availability of the Okimotos' *choojo*, Reiko, for an arranged marriage. The Okimotos, however, did not want their daughter to marry just yet. Mrs. Okimoto's head spun with anxiety as the matchmaker flipped through the folder of potential matches, names that she cross-referenced with a published registry of Japan's top one thousand income-earners. All of the eligible men, of course, came from households of wealth and/or political power. For his initial visit and for subsequent visits, the matchmaker received a gift of 30,000 yen (then about $150.00), and at the conclusion of the formal process of the *omiai,* he would receive ten times that amount.

Although Mrs. Okimoto seemed worried about the matchmaker, I heard little more about him or about marriage prospects until almost a full year after his first visit. In December 1980, Mrs. Okimoto and I planned to get together for dinner. As usual, she had made arrangements for her driver, Ikeda-san, to fetch me at my apartment. When he opened the rear door of the Okimotos' dark blue Cadillac, I was surprised to find the *okusama* waiting for me and noticed that she looked absolutely exhausted; heavy makeup only belied her pallor. I knew that she had just returned from a weekend in Seoul and wondered if something had gone wrong on her trip. The situation seemed even more puzzling when, as the car pulled out of the garage of my apartment building, the *okusama* turned to the driver and said, "Uchi wa taihen desu ne, Ikeda-san?" (Our household is in trouble, isn't it, Ikeda?). Something was taking a toll on Mrs. Okimoto's usual good cheer and health, and it soon became clear that it had nothing to do with her weekend jaunt.

On our way to her pied-à-terre in the center of the city, where we were to meet her husband for dinner, Mrs. Okimoto explained what was going on. She said that soon after the matchmaker had visited their home to present his portfolio, there came a request for an *omiai.* The Okimotos felt that their *choojo* was much too young for marriage; she was only twenty, after all, and had two more years of college to complete. However, they felt such an obligation to the matchmaker that they decided to go through with the *omiai,* fearing that an early refusal would offend the old man. Furthermore, they realized that an *omiai* did not necessarily mean marriage, and so they would go through the formalities of meeting and would figure out a way to refuse the proposal gracefully. *Okaasan* (Mother) and *Otoosan* (Father) discussed the matter with Reiko and presented it matter-of-factly: it was just a chance for her to practice. Reiko was a little nervous about the situation but immensely pleased.

Mrs. Okimoto said that she and her husband were unprepared, however, for the aggressiveness of the Hayashis, the prospective bridegroom's household. The Hayashis wanted their eldest son,

42

Tadashi, who was thirty, to marry immediately, and they thought Reiko would be the perfect *oyome-san* (young bride). The Hayashis, through the matchmaker, were relentless in their pursuit. They had, in fact, begun to draw up a list of guests for the engagement party, even before the final rounds of the *omiai* had been completed. Taken aback, the Okimotos asked for an *enki* (postponement in the final rounds of the talks).

In a lowered voice, Mrs. Okimoto continued to talk about her troubles. She said that the onslaught following the *omiai* forced her and her husband to consider not only Reiko's marriage but the whole future of their household: Who, in fact, would be next in line to fill the *ie*'s permanent positions of household head and household wife? Although the Okimotos were fond of their eldest son, the *choonan* (he was, and is, their pet), they really didn't believe that he had the talent or the temperament to *ato tsugu* (succeed in the household). As proof of his lack of merit, he had just entered a third-ranked university, best known for the number of foreign sports cars parked on its campus, while in comparison, Reiko was finishing her degree in the elite faculty of economics at one of the nation's most prestigious private universities. Even the two younger daughters were expected to follow in Reiko's footsteps. At the end of our quiet drive to dinner, Mrs. Okimoto said to me softly, "Anmari amayakasareta kara ne" (He was much too spoiled).

When we arrived at the Okimotos' apartment, we found the *shachoo* waiting impatiently for dinner to begin. He had some news about embarking on a new business venture but was unsure of his prospective partners, and so he was waiting for the *okusama* to recite their lineages, their *keitoo*. I was surprised that she could go back *sandai* (three generations) for each of the men about whom the *shachoo* was concerned. This talk of business and lineages quickly turned to the Okimotos' own household. The *shachoo* mentioned that many households were recruiting *muko-yooshi* among recent graduates of Tokyo University, the top-ranking national university.[7] Because such recruiting seemed calculating, the *shachoo* thought the phenomenon was simply awful. Mrs. Okimoto immediately replied that households must define an objective when it comes to marriage. For their household, she felt the objective was to bring in talent through marriage and adoption.* The *shachoo* looked directly at the *okusama* and calmly stated, "Sore wa so dake-do, shachoo wa iya" (That might be the case, but I [the president] am against it).[8]

As I listened to Mr. and Mrs. Okimoto, I recalled a conversation that I once had with Ba, the children's elderly nurse. In the kitchen of the main house one evening, Ba told me that the *shachoo* constantly reprimanded her for spoiling the *choonan*. She just couldn't help it. As Ba acknowledged her role in mismanaging the child's upbringing, she wondered aloud if the *okusama* would really consider bringing in a *muko-yooshi*. The *okusama*, who was within earshot, replied, "Other families have done it. We'll just split the business." Ba simply shook her head, said that such a situation would be sad indeed, and began to query me about whether or not professional matchmakers had much of a role in arranging marriages in the United States.

The *shachoo* and Ba were apparently not the only ones who preferred not to bring in a *muko-yooshi*. According to her mother, Reiko was also dead set against the idea. I had always assumed that it would be better for a young woman to remain in her household by bringing in a *muko-yooshi* than to go as an *oyome-san* to a strange household, where she would be subjected to a difficult life under the thumb of her mother-in-law. However, I was wrong. Mrs. Okimoto explained that she was asking a lot of her eldest daughter, for the young woman who brings in a *muko-yooshi* must not only

* W. Mark Fruin pointed out that in the family enterprise he studied, biological sons needed to provide evidence of merit, such as a graduate degree in economics or business from a Japanese or American university, in order to ensure them top positions in the enterprise. Fruin also made a keen observation about the relationship beween natural and adopted sons and their styles of management: "Natural sons and adopted sons are equally esteemed in the performance-conscious Japanese household system; but natural sons, because they have been reared and groomed in the environment of a family business, are perhaps too well informed and too well trained to take chances, to do things differently from their forebears, and generally to experiment with alternate products and processes. Adopted sons by contrast may be less reluctant to try something new; indeed they may have been anxious to prove their value with new ideas and innovative schemes. The two adopted sons who have been presidents in the postwar era were not adopted until they had completed their university training." *Kikkoman*, pp. 240–41.

44

assume the responsibility of training him in the ways of her household but must also bear the burden of mockery that is surely to be
encountered by marrying a man who is willing to give up the name
of his household for his bride's. The woman who brings in a *muko-
yooshi* not only keeps the household name but also inherits the
household property. She inherits the burden of a man. To bring
in a *muko-yooshi* means the denial of a lifelong dream, a dream of
becoming a true *hana-yome* (a newlywed bride), for if one brings in
a *muko-yooshi*, one is actually assuming the household headship in
the guise of the household wifeship; in essence, one is becoming
a man in the guise of a woman. To be put in such a position means
denying the very essence of femininity, and for these reasons,
women in such a position are often considered *kazoku no giseisha*,
sacrificial victims of their households. Reiko, therefore, saw the
prospect of marriage to Tadashi Hayashi, which her mother opposed, as her only chance to become a true *hana-yome*, her only
chance to escape becoming a *kazoku no giseisha*. She desperately
wanted to go to the Hayashi household as an *oyome-san*.

The Okimoto household was in turmoil. The *jijo* (second daughter) and the *sueko* (youngest child) were on Reiko's side. The *shachoo*
was angry with his wife for convincing him that the Okimoto
household needed to go through with this "practice" *omiai*. And
Mrs. Okimoto could barely stand the pain of realizing that her son
should not be the successor. He knew her opinion but how could
she talk to him about it? The position of household head needed
to be filled, and it was to be filled by merit and not by right of
birth.

Although in the Okimoto household both the *shachoo* and *okusama*
were considering the possibility of bringing in a nonkinsman successor through an uxorilocal marriage, the concept of patrilineal
descent remained a preferred strategy for household continuity.
Patrilineage is a cultural fact that figures in the way decisions are
made, and as a symbolic frame of reference, it serves as the foundation for life strategies within the *ie* and as a way of interpreting
life experiences. For the *shachoo*, the ideology of patrilineal descent
was important in his resistance to bringing in a talented nonkins-

man to succeed in the *ie*: to deny one's own son the position of household head seemed too calculating, too cold. For the *okusama*, the ideology of patrilineal descent made the decision to deny her eldest son a permanent position in the household extremely painful. It also molded Reiko's life expectations. She saw the prospect of remaining in her household of birth, of bearing the responsibility of the household lineage and property, not as a chance to have more control over her own life but as an immense burden, a sacrifice. It would deny her fulfillment as a woman.

The concept of patrilineal descent, therefore, structured the emotive response to, and meaning of, an important household event, an event in which parents were about to put aside their deep affection for their son and their consideration of their daughter's desire for fulfillment. They were to do all of this for the sake of the *ie*: *giri* would take precedence over *ninjoo*, duty over feeling. That shift in sensibility, that wrench to the heart, reveals the patterns of life in the *doozoku gaisha*, patterns of meaning, which develop from moment to moment, intricately.

The Okimotos' experience points to the very human actors who must staff the social organization of the *ie*. It is through the actions of individuals that the *ie* is reproduced in its original form over time. The *ie*, therefore, is not merely an organization but also a *normative* frame of reference, to which Japanese turn when they try to determine appropriate behavior. As a normative concept, the *ie* shapes the answer to the question: "What should I do or say?" And by acting on the answers to that question, men and women recreate and reproduce the *ie*, as a social organization, in perpetuity.

The *ie*, as a normative concept, works even more decisively to shape behavior between member and nonmember, insider and outsider, between groups. This can be seen in the transposition of the word *ie* itself: *uchi* (our household), *ie* (the household), and *otaku* (your household). The expression *uchi* is used in everyday speech to signify the school, company, household, or group to which one belongs. *Otaku* is an honorific form of address that signifies a person's group affiliation; it is an honorific form of "you." These transpositions of the concept of *ie* define membership, thereby serving as starting points for determining appropriate behavior between individuals as members of groups.[9]

The most basic kind of interaction between groups is giving and receiving—exchange. The appropriateness of the kind of exchange is determined through the normative frame of the *ie* and its manifestation in the forms of *uchi* and *otaku*. Through their choice of verbs and nouns, the Japanese communicate at least two things in their speech: verticality and distance. Within the group, or between hierarchically related groups, the humble, the informal/polite, and the exalted forms of words communicate status. One understands through even the most simple sentences the relative ranking of the speaker to the listener. One understands who is obligated to whom, who has power over whom. This is the communication of verticality. For example, when giving something to a status superior, one would use the verb *sashiagemasu* to denote "give" rather than *yarimasu*, which would be used to communicate giving something to a status subordinate. If one wanted to insult a status superior, all one would have to do is use *yarimasu* instead of *sashiagemasu*.

Distance is communicated in the same way. Exalted forms of verbs are used for those outside the *uchi*, whereas humble verb forms are used for those inside the *uchi*. In fact, it would be grammatically incorrect to use exalted forms of verbs when giving and receiving by an *uchi no hito*, one of "us," one of our household. Thus, while one would *sashiageru* (give) to *otaku* (you, your household), one could only *yaru* (give) to *uchi* (us, our household). Dorinne Kondo noted that this change of language when moving from *uchi* to *otaku* is linked to other patterns of behavior, from the way in which one carries the body to the way in which one dresses it: rough, informal language in the *uchi* corresponds to a relaxed carriage of the body, while precise, formal language corresponds to a more rigid carriage of the body and more formal dress at *otaku*.[10] The concept of *ie* creates a boundary defining membership, such that within the *uchi* informal involvement reigns, and outside the *uchi*, at *otaku*, a polite distance takes hold. "What is important here," Nakane wrote, "is that human relationships within the household group are thought of as more important than all other human relationships."[11]

The *uchi*, however, forms an extremely flexible yet absolutely precise boundary. For example, when two people are speaking with each other, they are *uchi* and *otaku*, but should a third person enter the conversation, the original two would have to decide consciously whether the third is the *otaku* in opposition to the original two, who might decide to form an *uchi*. This happens constantly in business situations, where two people of the same corporation but of different divisions are conversing. One treats the other as *uchi* toward *otaku*, but should a third person from *another* corporation enter the conversation, the original *uchi* and *otaku* unite as *uchi* and treat the newcomer as *otaku*. Samuel Martin writes: " 'In-group' and 'out-group' are flexible relative terms; when 'I give to you,' *you* are the out-group; but when 'you give to him,' *you* are absorbed in my in-group as opposed to *him*, unless he is an intimate of mine. When 'he gives to him,' we have to decide from the situation which of the two—*he* or *him*—is closer to *me* and belongs in the in-group."[12] This constant renegotiation is absolutely essential if one is to use the appropriate verb forms, if one is to speak grammatically, if one is to behave properly, and if one is to make one's allegiances clear. For the concept of *ie* to operate on the normative level, on the level of shaping appropriate speech and behavior, the *uchi* must be involved in the process of contextualization.

This process of contextualization brings us to another aspect of the *ie*: the *ie* as a cultural, as well as a normative, concept. David M. Schneider commented on the difference between cultural and normative questions: "Culture takes man's position vis-à-vis the world rather than *a* man's position on how to get along in the world as it is given; it asks 'Of what does this world consist?' where the normative level asks, 'Given the world to be made up in the way it is, how does a man proceed to act in it?' Culture concerns the stage, the stage setting, and the cast of characters; the normative system consists in the stage directions for the actors and how the actors should play their parts on the stage that is so set."[13]

In a universe consisting of relationships, the focal point is the *ie*, as the ever-contextualized *uchi*. The Japanese self does not relate to the Japanese other as I to You, as one individual to another individual, but as *uchi* to *otaku*, as a member of one group to a member of another group. Furthermore, the opposition between *uchi* and *otaku* disappears as the social context changes. This is how the Japanese see the universe, as a social, political, and economic field, wherein the *uchi* (us, who we are) is constantly negotiated.[14] Through this process of negotiation the Japanese come to understand themselves in opposition to foreigners in the context of the world; Osaka comes to understand itself in opposition to Tokyo in the context of cities in Japan; the downtown area, *shitamachi*, comes to understand itself in opposition to the middle-class suburban area, *yamanote*,[15] in the context of Tokyo neighborhoods; and so on. Jane Bachnik wrote:

> Two houses which are linked by ties of spatial proximity consider themselves basically in opposition and only when in opposition to another unit does the village become "we." Thus, in opposition to the village, the neighborhood views itself as "we," and only in opposition to the region the village is "we," and only in opposition to the "world" the Japanese are homogeneous and "we."
> Furthermore, all the different relationship categories are integrated into a single system at the level of the household members, who integrate and interpret them.[16]

The world, therefore, is the *uchi*, first in opposition to *otaku*, then combining with *otaku* to again form *uchi*, which is then in opposition to another *otaku*. In fact, the Japanese self comes to understand himself or herself, who he or she is, by being embedded in the *uchi*, the *uchi* in all of its configurations of oppositions and relationships in the various contexts of human life.

We know who the characters in the play are by their place in the set, the contextualized *uchi*, but what are they? Dorinne Kondo suggested that the answer lies in another cultural aspect of the *ie*, the *ie* as form as opposed to the *uchi* as feeling.[17] The *ie* is a set of positions and roles, a social world bound by duties, rights, and obligations. It is, in fact, outer form, which manifests itself in *giri*, social obligations. The concept of *ie* is behind the force that makes individuals recognize and observe moral and ethical codes of conduct so that the social institution of the household is maintained, irrespective of how an individual might feel about those with whom he or she must interact or about the rules he or she must obey. The *ie*, as outer form, embraces authority and formality. The *ie* is reason based on social needs, and as such, it is a frame of mind. In sharp contrast to the *ie* is the *uchi*, the family, the rough-and-tumble center of warmth, acceptance, emotional depth, the locus of the heart. *Ie* is to *giri*, obligations, as *uchi* is to *ninjoo*, the realm of deep personal feelings. In the *uchi*, personal inclinations can be draped about like the stockings hanging from the bidet in the bathroom reserved for, and seen only by, *uchi no hito*, members of the family.

I saw the *ie* and *uchi* carried about in the minds and hearts of my informants, wherever they went. Mrs. Moriuchi, for example, always amused me with her *ie* appropriateness and her *uchi* antics. Her family is a *bunke* (branch) of an *ie* that builds machinery, and since her husband's death she has felt especially obligated to the *honke* (main family) for financial and social support. She would continue to need such support until a decision could be made as to who would succeed in her branch family. Indeed, she hoped that her son would take over the leadership of the *bunke*. Failing that, she felt that she could count on one of her daughters to bring in a suitable *muko-yooshi*. In a restaurant one evening, she, her son, her eldest daughter, and I were surprised by a visit to our private dining room by the *honke no okusama* (wife of the main family). After the maître d' announced her arrival, we pulled ourselves out from under the *kotatsu* (a table set over a heated area) and prepared ourselves for the ritual of bowing and exchanging greetings. Toward the end of the brief exchange, Mrs. Moriuchi said, "Uchi wa itsumo osewa ni natte orimasu no de . . ." (Our family is always such a burden on you . . .). After the *honke no okusama* left the room, Mrs. Moriuchi turned her face toward the entrance, and her perfectly elegant, oval face, defined by high, thin eyebrows, turned into a cross-eyed mask replete with a fervently wagging tongue. We all roared with laughter and proceeded to get drunk. I witnessed, in those few moments, the strict observance of a social obligation on the part of the *bunke* toward the *honke* in the context of the *ie* and the irreverence of personal inclinations in the context of the *uchi*.

The comic nature of the evening with Mrs. Moriuchi highlights the seriousness of the *ie*/*uchi*, form/feeling, *giri*/*ninjoo* oppositions as cultural concepts. The *ie*/*uchi* distinction is a defining dimension of the Japanese self; it answers the question: What am I? For the Japanese, the self is outer form as well as inner feeling, social obligation as well as personal inclination. By participating in the *ie* and *uchi*, the Japanese comes to understand himself or herself as partly societal and partly personal; he or she comes to understand that the joining of the societal and the personal leads to fulfillment and that the parting of *giri* and *ninjoo* can only lead to tragedy. The *ie*/*uchi* distinction, as a cultural concept, orders the Japanese self by defining what society expects and how the individual feels. The *ie*, as the frame of mind, and the *uchi*, as the locus of the heart, are just as real as Mrs. Moriuchi bowing in deep obligation one moment and wagging her tongue the very next.

Thus, by uttering the words *uchi*, *ie*, and *otaku* every day, the Japanese cross various experiential planes: cultural, normative, social organizational, and even physical, for the words *uchi*, *ie*, and *otaku* literally mean house. By uttering the words every day, by using them to determine behavior, by having them set life's stage, by participating in the *ie* and *uchi* through birth and death as members of the household and the family, one touches the very core, indeed the essence, of life. And that, perhaps, is why the *ie* has such a tenacious hold on Japanese society.

4 DEATH

In the *ie*'s strength as a design for living lies its greatest problem, one that is most pressing in life within the large-scale family
enterprise. Within the boundary of the *doozoku gaisha* two distinct
planes of reality, the familial and the economic, are held together
by the concept of the *ie*. Yet it is very clear that familial needs and
attachments do not necessarily coincide with rational economic
interests. There are, in fact, ambiguities that arise from the integration of these two planes, as in the case of the dearly loved eldest
son who is not competent enough to head the enterprise. What
happens to the family's feelings of love, bitter disappointment, and
hate? We must look at two more realms of reality that are encom-
passed by the *ie*: the rational and the nonrational, the cognitive
and the emotive. What is thought to be good for the enterprise
may not feel right for the family. Yet the enterprise and the family
are one in the *ie*. How do members of the household approach real
dilemmas in their lives? What provides the framework for the res-
olution of problems? What provides the framework for action?

We begin to answer these questions by looking at an experience
that *must be shared* by everyone, an experience that is absolutely
inescapable: death in the household. By coming to terms with
death, men and women of the *doozoku gaisha* develop a symbolic
framework that is, at once, cognitive and emotive and that can be

shared and used collectively to resolve the dilemmas of life, to understand, to adapt, to innovate, and to create.

Ghosts in General

At the end of the nineteenth century, Baron Nobushige Hozumi, a noted observer of Japanese customs, took great pleasure in seeing Henry Irving play Hamlet at the Lyceum Theatre in London. However, he had one point of criticism:

> Hamlet, as represented by Irving, appeared to me as constantly showing signs of fear and dread, not only on account of the horrible story told by his father's ghost—which is but natural—but for the ghost itself. A Japanese actor, if he were to act the part of Hamlet, would certainly show strong marks of love and respect towards the father's spirit, mingled with the feeling of sorrow and sympathy for his father's spirit, and of horror and anger at the "foul and most unnatural murder." He would perhaps try to embrace the phantom instead of parrying, as the great English actor did. Of course, I by no means say that this is the proper way of representing Shakespeare's famous play; nor do I presume to think that I understood Irving's acting well. I only state my impression. Ghost scenes are not uncommon in Japanese theatres; and when the ghost appears to the parents, sons, daughters, friends or lovers, those who meet never show signs of dread, but those of joy for the meeting, mingled perhaps with sorrow and sympathy.[1]

This impression led Hozumi to conclude that "the theory of the 'dread of ghosts' and 'ghost-propitiation' seems unnatural so far as the worship of ancestors is concerned; and, however strange the expression may sound to Western ears, I deem it nearer the truth to say that it was the *'Love of Ghosts'* which gave rise to the custom of ancestor-worship."[2]

A Ghost in the Graveyard

In early July 1981, Hasegawa-sensei, a high-ranking Buddhist priest, thought he had seen a ghost on the grounds of his temple. He had been in his study when he saw a figure enter the temple

54

graveyard. Hasegawa-sensei knew that it was a bit too early for *obon mukai*, when family members gather at their household's *ohaka* (tomb) to greet their ancestors as they return to the world of the living for *obon* (Festival of the Dead). The thought of ghosts emerged from his childhood in the delirium of heat, humidity, and overwork. Summoning his courage, Hasegawa-sensei went into the graveyard and found a young woman talking to a tombstone. Startled, she burst into tears. Later, in Hasegawa-sensei's study, the young woman began to tell him that she was deeply troubled. She was of marriageable age, yet none of her *omiai* had gone well because she had been stricken with a mysterious disease. Furthermore, no doctor could diagnose it. She was terribly confused. All she knew was that she wasn't well, and as a result she could probably neither marry nor have children. The young woman had come to her household grave to ask her ancestors to pardon her for being unfilial because of her failure at marriage. She also came to ask them their forgiveness for taking her own life. She was on the verge of suicide.

Hasegawa-sensei walked her back to her home and asked her to visit a friend of his, a doctor, the very next morning. The doctor called Hasegawa-sensei the next day to say that he could find nothing wrong with the young woman, but that he did prescribe something: she was to go to the temple every day at 6 A.M. to pray and to meditate for an hour until all her symptoms had disappeared. Hasegawa-sensei felt compelled to join in her morning prayers.[3]

A few days later, I visited Hasegawa-sensei's temple to witness *segaki-kuyoo*, a mass for the dead.

"Yare, yare," sighed Hasegawa-sensei, wiping the perspiration from the rolls of fat under his chin.

Obon was an impossibly difficult time for him. His wicker sleeve guard[4] clicked against a Cartier wristwatch as he pointed to photos of his prize-winning Yorkshire terriers and their trophies; he had hardly had any time at all to care for them during the past two weeks. Aside from attending to his ceremonial duties, he had been compelled to get up at 5 A.M. to prepare for morning prayers with the unfortunate young woman. (I never found out what eventually happened to her.) He felt overwhelmed by this kind of work—*katei soodan*, giving advice, much like a family therapist. People had been calling him morning, noon, and night to discuss household issues: problems of succession to the household headship, litanies of suffering from maligned daughters-in-law, threats of suicide from "unfilial" sons and daughters. Maybe, he speculated, it was simply statistical, for there were over one thousand parishioners in his temple, and since everyone has problems. . . . But these problems always seem to surface during *obon*.

"The truth of the matter," he said, "is that all eyes are focused on the spirits of the dead."

People look to the *kokoro* (hearts, spirits, or souls) of their household *hotokesama* (dead) during *obon*, which makes them reflect on their present lives. In fact, Hasegawa-sensei stressed that this process of reflection during *obon* is one of self-understanding, and *obon* serves as a medium for heightening the experience of self-understanding. Through *obon*, one focuses on the souls of the dead and comes to an understanding of one's *joosoo*, one's existence in the realm of sentiments and personal attachments, in its present state as a particular manifestation of its entire historical development. In other words, one lives with one's past.

One's past, furthermore, is embodied in the *ie*. Jane Bachnik explained:

> Since the household is not an individual, but a group frame of reference, the members share in a very essential sense elements of a common "biography" since they share social reference coordinates for interpretation of their ongoing experiences, as "history."
>
> The household is like a strip of movie film in which each generation sees itself as part of the whole strip in space/time. *Ie* concerns the entire time/space trajectory of the household; *uchi* focuses on the present occupants of the household in close-up. The previous and future generations of the household are assumed in *uchi* as well, but they are not its focus, which is rather the present "frame" of the ongoing movie of the household in time/space. This relation of the individual to the group defines both the obligation to succeed the group, or to sustain the household "line" without ceasing. It also defines the parameters of intragroup decision-making.[5]

Because the history of the *ie* serves as the interpretive frame for experiences of the *uchi*, the household's past is a prologue to behavior in the temporal present, in the *uchi*.

From my experience with *obon* and from my informant's accounts of experiences with death and dying, I came to understand that life strategies are intimately connected with the past, the past as an ordered succession of generations, as well as an ordered interpretation of death within the household. History, therefore, is death in the *ie* giving way to life in the *uchi*, the past informing the present. How is the past structured as prologue?

The answer begins with Hasegawa-sensei's deep regard for ritual, which he believes is the most important aspect of life in human society. Without ritual, life becomes meaningless for the individual. With every important life-cycle event, there is a ceremony: birth, marriage, and death are all ritualized. "Isn't it through that kind of ritualization that intensification of experience takes place?" he asked rhetorically.

Through a cycle of rituals revolving around birth, auspicious events, and death, self-consciousness is awakened, the consciousness of self as part of *fushi* (eternal life), of being connected to the past and the future. Hasegawa-sensei went on to complain vehemently that human beings are terribly weak and cannot assume the responsibility of *fushi* on their own. In fact, human beings can't even be expected to remember their *hotokesama*, their household dead, which is a crucial, yet simple, task in awakening, and maintaining, the consciousness of self as part of *fushi*. "If it weren't for *obon* and the work of priests, one would forget one's own mother and father only two or three days after death. That kind of forgetting is extremely dangerous, for one loses an understanding of the self."

Obon, apparently, is an antidote for that kind of carelessness. *Obon*, like all other cultural artifacts, according to Hasegawa-sensei, is based on a crude kind of rationality, that is, the necessity of human beings to organize their lives, to be placed in history, to abide by the rules of heaven and society. "Without them, one carelessly forgets," Hasegawa-sensei warned, toying absentmindedly with one of his terriers' trophies. One carelessly forgets how to participate in, and create, a meaningful existence, an existence bound in heaven, society, and history.

Obon, therefore, is crucial to the understanding of the past as

57

prologue, for the Festival of the Dead is a time when a family comes to see itself as a particular outcome of its *ie*'s history, when present patterns in the *uchi* are seen as outgrowths of the household's past. *Obon*, furthermore, occurs in the *uchi*, where ancestors-cum-gods mingle with the living, where the realm of the sacred blends with the profane. *Obon*, in essence, imbues the quintessentially mundane, that is, the concern with household histories, with an otherworldly quality. I shall examine the place of *obon* in ancestral rites and the place of ancestor worship in the structure of the household. I shall also look at the participants in ancestral rites and consider to what extent they believe or disbelieve in ancestors and spirits and how their belief or disbelief might actually affect behavior in the household.

Transforming the Dead

Obon in Tokyo begins on July 13.[6] On temple grounds and in their homes, families are busy with preparations to welcome the spirits of the household dead back to their homes. Tombstones are cleaned. Flowers and offerings of food are placed before them. On the evening of the thirteenth, living members of the household walk to the temple graveyard to welcome home the dead: at the household tomb the spirits are greeted and guided home with a lantern embossed with the household crest, but more often than not, the dead are led with simple paper lanterns bought at the very last minute at a local convenience store. At home, the flame from the lantern is transferred to a candle on a specially constructed *obon* altar. On July 16, the flame is transferred back to the lantern, and the dead are walked back to the household tomb, where they return to the spirit world. For those families who live beyond walking distance from their temple grounds, a *mukaebi* (welcoming fire) of dried hemp stalks is lighted on the thirteenth, and an *okuribi* (send-off fire) is lighted on the sixteenth to wish Godspeed to the spirits on their journey between the realms of the living and the dead. Although *obon* is an important event, it is only one part of the whole ritual cycle that revolves around caring for the dead.

"The mental process evolving from the memorial services," Herman Ooms pointed out, "contains something more than merely keeping the memory of the deceased alive. It is as much one of remembering as forgetting." In fact, *obon* and other memorial rites are part of a highly ordered process of forgetting, whereby the deceased move in stages from the status of departed to that of ancestorhood, as they are gradually expunged from the memories of the living. This ordered, extremely regular, process of forgetting takes the dead through the following status transformation: from *shiryoo* (spirits of the newly deceased) to *nii-botoke* (new buddhas); from *nii-botoke* to *hotoke* (buddhas); and finally, from *hotoke* to *senzo* (ancestors-cum-gods).[7] Although the priest Hasegawa decried the human tendency of forgetting the dead, the process of transforming the dead from *shiryoo* to *senzo* means that at some point in time the living will let go of, will indeed forget, the dead—but without a sense of guilt.

Transforming the dead is the work of the living, and it begins with a series of funerary and memorial events, which serve to cleanse the *shiryoo* of the pollution of death. Until members of the household have aided in separating the *shiryoo* from direct involvement with life, it remains a source of danger for the living. "The spirit of the newly dead," according to Robert J. Smith,

> remains something of a threat to the living, at least until the first *bon* [*obon*] following death. Then it is welcomed back to the house with special greetings and offerings that are usually placed on an altar separate from that for the ancestral spirits. Often referred to as "new buddha" (*nii-botoke*) until sent away with all the other ancestors at the end of its first *bon*, the *shirei* [*shiryoo*] retains some of the contamination of death that must be ritually cleansed.
>
> When a member of the household dies, the immediate concern is to begin the process of removing his spirit from the realm of daily life and ultimately from the entire world of men.[8]

Until the *shiryoo* is removed from worldly concerns, there is a fear of *tatari* (curses) by the *shiryoo* that may be incurred if he or she is thought to have been maligned in life. Thus, there is a sense in which the dead must be appeased by living members of the household.

On a winter evening in 1980, I witnessed for the first time the interaction between the living and the dead, when I dropped by at the Moriuchis for a chat. Their low, rambling home always seemed peculiarly *sabishii* (empty and lonely). Makoto, the Moriuchis' second child and only son, showed me into the dining room, where I found the *okusama* and Nobuko, the eldest daughter, huddled at one corner of a dining table that would seat twenty comfortably. Akiko, the youngest child, was at a meeting of her high school music club.

Twin baby grands sat at the other end of the room. Black and highly polished, they were silent, disturbing reminders of days when the house was bursting with guests. Although Akiko practiced regularly, Makoto and Nobuko would hardly touch the pianos now, for the silly tunes they played only took them back to scenes of their father and mother singing off-key to their friends, as they prepared to fly off to Okinawa in the south for a beach holiday: Daddy's treat. When I got to know the Moriuchis, it had been five years since his death.

When I entered the dining room, Nobuko ran up to me, forgoing the formal greetings, so that she could immediately pluck at my clothing. She was always fascinated by my labels from department stores in Boston, for they absolutely established me as a "foreigner" to her, in contrast to my Japanese face. The *okusama*, on the other hand, greeted me formally, scolded Nobuko for being bad mannered, and proceeded to close an open cabinet, after blowing out the votive candles contained within it. I had not noticed the cabinet before. I caught glimpses of a photo, flowers, and other objects. My curiosity was piqued.

After the *okusama* retired, I asked Makoto to show me the inside of the cabinet. He seemed pleased. We walked up to it, and on opening the doors, he immediately introduced me to his father. "Hajimemashite" (Nice to meet you), I heard myself say to a photo of Makoto's deceased father. Makoto snickered. I didn't know quite what to make of the situation, and so I asked about the objects in the cabinet: a photo, a vase with flowers, an *ihai* (a memorial tablet with the deceased's posthumous name written on the front and the predeath name on the back), a porcelain bowl with ashes for lighting incense, votive candles, a brass container shaped like an eggcup with cooked rice in it, a little dish of fruit, and a miniature bottle of Johnnie Walker Black Label scotch.

"Father likes to drink," Makoto explained. He talked about his father in the present tense, as if he were alive. In fact, the Moriuchis had just finished sharing their evening meal with Mr. Moriuchi when I walked in.

I had not noticed the cabinet earlier because it was always closed and its doors were exactly like an entire bank of doors in polished blonde wood, which were built into the dining room wall and behind which were stored books and records. This particular cabinet, however, turned out to be a makeshift *butsudan* (ancestral altar). The most common kind of *butsudan* is a standing cabinet, wherein the *ihai* are kept. *Butsudan* also have a lower drawer, which usually holds certificates, family documents, and other important papers. The *butsudan* can be rather elaborate, and in the Okimoto household, it took up an entire wall, the upper half occupied by the cabinet and the lower half by an antique safe, of a kind I had previously seen only in classic cowboy movies. But the *butsudan* at the Moriuchis' simply occupied a convenient cupboard. I asked why they hadn't purchased a standard *butsudan*, and Makoto replied that their present home might not be the final resting place for his father, for the *ihai* might be transferred to the *butsudan* at the *honke* (main family), where his grandfather's *ihai* was kept and venerated. Furthermore, he said, it would be a bad omen to buy a *butsudan*, for it would seem as if one were preparing for more deaths in the home.

Nobuko bounded in at this point and asked if she could make us a few stiff gin and tonics, but she got caught up in our conversation and forgot about the drinks for a while. She began poking around the cabinet, saying that there should be photographs of her father's funeral somewhere. She finally dug them out from under a pile of phonograph records in another cabinet. We sat at the dining room table, silently poring over the photographs.

Nobuko broke the silence: "It progressed on its own, almost automatically, didn't it, Makoto?" Nobuko explained that the whole series of events seemed to have moved on their own; it didn't feel much like her father's funeral services at all; she felt as if she were just an actress in a clearly defined play—someone was always giving her instructions, directing her actions.

"I felt as if I were simply cast adrift in the ritual aspects of the funeral," Nobuko said softly. The entire event had impressed Nobuko with its beauty. The head priest from the temple, which the Moriuchi household patronized, appeared to direct the services. Dressed in robes of gold and wearing the Moriuchi crest, he set the tone for an atmosphere of elegance: the smell of flowers, the deep sound of sutras intoned, the veil of smoking incense. Everything seemed so strangely beautiful and mystifying. Nobuko forgot her sorrow.

Makoto, on the other hand, thought that from the moment his father died, the situation was politically charged, and that is why he could hardly think of his sorrow. He pointed out that it was simply naive to think that all those events moved on their own: there were people behind the movement. A whole cast of characters suddenly entered the play, as it were. Nobuko's and Makoto's father was the third son of a family of five siblings, or six if one counted the last son born to their grandfather's recognized *omekake-san* (mistress). And all of the surviving members and their hired staff appeared. Makoto remembered his Uncle Masao, his father's elder brother and second son of that generation, appearing at their home with his personal secretary, just as Yodogawa-san, Makoto's father's *nyoobo-yaku* (the man who plays the role of a "wife" to the company president; the most trusted assistant) appeared with *his* personal secretary. There was extreme anxiety surrounding that meeting, for Uncle Masao had intended to take charge of the whole funeral. He felt that as president of Moriuchi Industries, the *oya-gaisha* (main enterprise) of the Moriuchi household, he should be completely responsible. Yodogawa-san, on the other hand, felt that the funeral should be the responsibility of Moriuchi Science and Technology, a *kogaisha* (subsidiary), of which Makoto's father had been president. The tension broke with Makoto's mother calmly stating her desire that Moriuchi Science and Technology handle all the arrangements. There had long been bad feeling between the faction that Uncle Masao heads and the faction that Makoto's late father used to head. Thus, if Yodogawa-san and Makoto's mother had allowed Uncle Masao to handle all the arrangements, it would have amounted to a public concession to Uncle Masao's power and an acceptance of his authority.

The funeral services were just another arena in which the hostility within the Moriuchi household could be acted out. The families and their enterprises within the *ie* had been on bad terms since Makoto's grandfather, the founder of Moriuchi Industries, had died without naming a successor. The families fought about which one should be the main family, the *honke*, and which ones would be relegated to the status of *bunke*, branch families. The hostility was extreme.

By not allowing Uncle Masao to participate directly in the planning of the funeral, Makoto's family and its staff took away the possibility for Uncle Masao to appease Makoto's much-maligned father in death. Denied the opportunity to be among those members of the *ie* who directly care for the newly dead, Uncle Masao was shut out from the process of relieving himself of the anxiety created by his younger brother's accusation that Masao had tried to undermine his leadership of Moriuchi Science and Technology. Uncle Masao was condemned to live with the guilt of his misdeeds and the threat of *tatari*.

Nobuko had been listening silently to Makoto, but she frowned at this point and asked him why he felt it necessary to force everyone to return to these awful memories. Nobuko jumped up from the table, headed for the bar to finally make the gin and tonics, and ordered Makoto and me to ready ourselves to go out dancing in Roppongi: "Let's get going! Makoto, you're *such* a weird kid." Looking sheepishly at Nobuko, then at me, Makoto apologized quietly, "Gomen ne, oneechama" (I'm sorry, Big Sister). Assuming a girlish and childlike voice, Makoto suddenly seemed too young to join Nobuko and me on our night on the town.

It had been five years since Mr. Moriuchi's death, yet his presence in the home was still clearly felt by the *okusama* and his children. He had become a memory, yet they spoke about him in the present tense and even introduced me to him, as a new friend of theirs. It became clear to me that the separation of Mr. Moriuchi's soul from direct involvement with the living could not have occurred abruptly with the performance of a certain ritual or the passing of a certain date. The separation had to be gradual. Yet in Japanese memorial rites there are clear markers of separation, and the most important of these are: the funeral, the forty-ninth-day ceremony, and the first *obon*, or *nii-bon*.

"Once the memory of the deceased is abolished," Ooms wrote,

> his individuality will have disappeared, but he will be a full member of the ancestor half of the *ie* and no more subject to change. This transition, however, moves smoothly and does not involve such an abrupt change as the one which occurs at the funeral or the 49th day. That there is a marked difference between the status of the soul before and after the 49th day is clear from the following. Although the soul in a certain sense is believed to be in the house all the time . . . , the household members experience two periods of intense presence: the time until the 49th day and during *Obon*. But the former is marked by a state of uncertainty and uneasiness while the latter is definitely one of joy, and a cautious attitude is completely missing—notice that the 49th day and the first *Obon* may follow each other closely. Both relate to the soul but at different times and at a different stage of development.[9]

Death for Makoto Moriuchi seemed a strange thing, barely explicable: "You know, even if one dies, it doesn't mean that one does not exist. Maybe that's why I'm not afraid of death." After his father died, there were two days of wake, the *kari-tsuya* and the *hon-tsuya*. He admitted that he felt like his sister during that period, simply swept away by the events. That feeling lasted through the *missoo* (funeral ceremony) on the third day after his father's death. On that day, Makoto remembered, his seemingly blurred vision cleared; he felt a sharpening of his senses as the funeral ended and as members of the family proceeded to the *kasooba* (crematorium). The vision of going to the *kasooba* to participate in putting his father's cremated remains into the *kotsu tsubo* (urn for bones) still haunts him occasionally.[10]

What Makoto recalled most vividly was the moment the attendant pulled a tray from the crematory, on which lay an indistinct figure of a man. It was his father. It was shocking. He felt extremely *sabishii*, lonely and empty. Then the attendant gave the tray a shake, and in an instant the figure crumbled into shapeless dust and shards of bone. It was an amazing experience, for in a split second he saw his father turn into something that was still his father, but wasn't. At this point in his recollection, Makoto began to stumble over his words, for he couldn't quite remember how he had felt. It was all so odd. In that very instant, his father had become a memory. Yet it was much more concrete than a memory, for a few seconds after the tray was shaken, he was picking pieces of bone out of the ash with Nobuko and transferring them into the *kotsu tsubo*. Their younger sister, Akiko, still in elementary school at that time, was spared the task.

"And that's why," he explained, "people are so shocked when they see two foreigners helping each other pick up food with chopsticks. When two people pick up a single piece of food in unison with two pairs of chopsticks, it reminds them of this. It's horrifying."

But it really didn't feel as if he were picking up pieces of his father and transferring them into a jar. Makoto felt as if he were actually creating a memory of him in a very concrete way, creating something that was to represent his father. After the *kotsu tsubo* was brought home, he and Akiko would stare quietly at it. But he often heard his mother and Nobuko sobbing, talking to the *kotsu tsubo*, as if it were his father. Again, he felt as if it really were his father, yet it wasn't. His father's death, Makoto told me, neither frightened him nor made him extremely sad; instead, he felt abandoned and terribly lonely. *Sabishii.*

On the forty-ninth day after the death of Makoto's father, the entire household, including Uncle Masao, gathered at the household tomb that was established by Makoto's grandfather in Tokyo. It was *nookotsu*, the ceremony in which the *kotsu tsubo* is laid to rest. Some of the emotional intensity surrounding his father's death had dissipated. On the drive to the graveyard, Makoto, Nobuko, and the *okusama* had a brief discussion about the *kotsu tsubo*, while Akiko listened in an uninterested manner. Mrs. Moriuchi informed her children that she had been thinking of establishing a separate tomb, but for the time being, laying their father to rest in the household tomb didn't seem like such a bad idea. If, however, Uncle Masao continued to irritate her, the *okusama* intended to take the *kotsu tsubo* out of the tomb and establish her own, effectively starting up an independent *bunke*, that is, starting up a new household.

About Mr. Moriuchi's bones, the *okusama* remarked matter-of-factly, "We can take them out anytime." To Makoto this kind of discussion seemed a clear sign that life was returning to the mundane. Indeed, it was a return to the mundane world of family feuds, but now there was an important difference: the deceased was an *indirect* participant. For the Moriuchi household, the forty-ninth-day ceremony meant that the remains of the deceased were placed in the household tomb, and what was brought back from that ceremony to the world of the living, to the home, was the *ihai* (memorial tablet). The separation of the *ihai* from the *kotsu tsubo* was the final separation of the spirit from the corpse. This separation signified the transition of the spirit of the newly dead to the status of new buddha. It also signified the removal of Mr. Moriuchi from *direct* participation in the world of the living and opened the way for his *indirect* participation as a household *hotokesama*. Because living members of the household questioned the placement of Mr. Moriuchi's urn in the household tomb, he became a potential point of symbolic and emotional contention. If his urn were removed from the household tomb, the act would be a statement of rebellion: an *uchi* breaking away from the *ie*, thereby establishing a completely new household. It would be a case of indirect participation by the dead with real-life consequences.

During those first forty-nine days after Mr. Moriuchi's death, when the status of his soul changed from *shiryoo* to *nii-botoke*, the living members of his household participated in this transition; they also transformed their relationship with him, from one with the living to one with the dead. In the movie strip of the *ie*, Mr. Moriuchi's active presence in the divisions and the emotional life of the household was placed one frame in the past. With his death, the movie strip moved one frame forward, and Mr. Moriuchi was carried beyond his death by living members of the *ie*, so that he participated in the events of the temporal present as a symbolic point of love and contention, to which living members referred in their attempt to understand and to *alter* their life situations. By adjusting to his death, the surviving members of the household did not eliminate Mr. Moriuchi from their lives. Instead, they opened the way for Mr. Moriuchi's continued presence in the household: from flesh and blood to a symbol of love and hate.

Transforming the Living

During those forty-nine days of transition, the Moriuchis were not only intensely involved in adjusting to Mr. Moriuchi's changing status but they were also actively reaffirming their statuses vis-à-vis one another. The first few days after Mr. Moriuchi's death were the most emotionally trying and tense. With his death, the entire *ie* needed to be realigned, but this realignment was not clear-cut, for no one was quite sure who was the head of the household, and therefore, the rearrangement of positions within the household could not proceed in an orderly fashion. No one could judge his or her position relative to other household members because there was no stable point of reference: no single *uchi* was clearly the *honke*. This confusion and its inherent struggle manifested itself in a rigid adherence to birth order in functions that were open to the public. In reception lines, for example, mourners first encountered the family of procreation—Mrs. Moriuchi, Makoto, the only son, Nobuko, the eldest daughter, and finally Akiko—then the deceased's brothers, with the *choonan* (eldest brother) first, the *jinan* (second eldest) second, and so on. However, in the private, informal gatherings, reserved only for members of the household, their personal staff, and intimates, status determined by birth order was deliberately undermined. For example, at informal meals following each ceremony, each of the brothers wanted to claim the seat of most importance, the *kamiza*, thereby establishing himself as the symbolic head of the household, but because no one quite dared, they instead scattered about in a random fashion and forced their embarrassed hired subordinates, their personal staff, to occupy the seats of highest status.

A similar status struggle occurred in the Itoo household when Mitsuko Nishimura's grandfather died. That struggle involved the women of the household and focused on the presence of Mitsuko's young aunt, Toyoko (Otoyo) Itoo, whose joie de vivre only I seemed to have fully appreciated.

"You know my Aunt Otoyo, the one we don't like," began Mitsuko.

"I didn't know that you didn't like her," I replied.

"Well, it's not that I don't like her, but she is a rather sad creature. I feel sorry for her. My mother and my aunts really have been unkind to her."

Mitsuko's grandfather had married twice, his first wife having died young. Aunt Otoyo was the wife of the eldest son from the first marriage. He always laid claim to the successorship of the Itoo household, a claim that only Aunt Otoyo recognized. Indeed, Aunt Otoyo's husband headed a subsidiary in the Itoo network of businesses, and Mitsuko's father, the *choonan* from her grandfather's second marriage, headed the main enterprise.

Aunt Otoyo was a relatively new member of the Itoo household, for she, too, was a second wife. In order to marry her, Mitsuko's uncle had had to divorce his first wife, whom he detested and would never have married were it not for his father's orders. At the time of the divorce, Mitsuko's uncle proclaimed his love for Otoyo to his family. This act was a source of embarrassment to the Itoos, for it revealed a terrible weakness in character. It seemed impulsive and adolescent to Mitsuko's father and mother. Her grandfather stopped speaking to her uncle after he married Otoyo.

Mitsuko's uncle, furthermore, chose to fall in love with a woman of distinctly lower socioeconomic status. Her natal household owned a medium-sized enterprise that had gone bankrupt, and since the Itoos married only *meimon no kazoku* (illustrious households), this union was a blemish. The women of the Itoo household feared that Otoyo was merely enamored of the Itoo name and might be, in fact, extremely ambitious and potentially dangerous.

Thus, the *okusama* of the various families that ran businesses in the Itoo household united to shut Otoyo out. They began their campaign by treating her as a woman of immensely lower status. For example, when Otoyo was first introduced to her new nephews and nieces, she was not introduced as *obasama* (Aunt). She was introduced by her given name. Because household structure is premised on positions, not individuals, one's positional title is more important than one's personal name. In fact, by referring to someone within the household by his or her personal name rather than a kinship term, one insults the person, directly and obviously. Such an act means the exclusion of the person from the group. If, for example, one did not like one's older sister's husband, one could make it clear by referring to him and addressing him with his family name + *san*, "Mr. So and So," rather than *oniisama* (Older Brother).[11] Otoyo's case of terminological exclusion was even more severe, for they introduced her as "Otoyo-san." The other *okusama* shortened her given name, Toyoko, to *Toyo*, then added *O* before it and *san* after: *O* + *Toyo* + *san*. That is what one does with the names of one's maids.

The final and clearest act of exclusion came at the funeral service for Mitsuko's grandfather. Traditionally, in the lighting of incense during funeral services, strict birth order is followed: from the oldest son to the youngest, then the daughters, oldest to youngest; spouses follow immediately. Well, before the services began, the wives of the Itoo household banded together and told Otoyo that she was not to follow her husband in the incense lighting; rather, her turn would come after all the guests had finished. Otoyo was unmistakably placed outside the household—thrown out. Before the eyes of the public she became a *kanzen na tanin* (complete outsider). This, of course, infuriated Otoyo. She was to have her revenge later.

The events of the funerals in the Moriuchi and Itoo households provided family members with an array of symbolic weapons with which to wage their status wars. By participating in the funerary rites, they not only came to understand, perforce, their positions within the structure and dynamics of the *ie* but they also used these rites to stake out those positions.

The forty-ninth day marks the end of mourning,[12] the end of a period of major transition and potential upheaval within the *ie*. It is no wonder that the end of this period is generally called *imi-ake* (the lifting of pollution). The communal sigh of relief, however, does not come until *nii-bon*, the first Festival of the Dead to be celebrated after a death in the household. Ooms pointed out that the forty-ninth day ceremony is still marked by uncertainty and uneasiness, while *obon* is a joyous occasion. They both relate to the spirit of the dead but at different stages of its development.[13] *Nii-bon* marks a time when the newly deceased is finally sent off to the spirit world, when it is finally separated from direct involvement in the world of the living.

Every Household a Temple

On that hot July afternoon in 1981, Hasegawa-sensei explained to me that I was about to witness an event that combined two things: *segaki-kuyoo*, a general mass for the dead, and *nii-bon no kuyoo*, a mass for those who had died since the last *obon*. Although the English translation of *segaki* is "mass for the dead," Hasegawa-sensei informed me that the characters mean *gaki ni hodokosu* (give to, or bestow upon, the hungry ghosts). This mass, held on July 10, is the most important event of the *obon* period. "The atmosphere of the ceremony shows everyone that we are extremely close to the world of the dead," he remarked.

This feeling of closeness to death is combined with a sense of charity for those hungry ghosts, the *gaki*, who have no household attachments and are left unattended by the living. Without offerings of food and drink and without offerings of prayer, they are caught between the worlds of the living and the dead. Hungry ghosts, like other wandering spirits, are "stuck." The distinction between the wandering spirits and those that have household attachments can be seen in the special *obon* altars that are set up in homes. Smith described two of them, "one for the ancestral spirits and one for the wandering ghosts. With the one, benign spirits of the ancestors, the object of daily and periodic worship, are summoned back to the world of the living to participate for a short time in the festivities; with the other, wandering spirits, potentially harmful because they are homeless and unworshiped by their descendants, are fed and comforted in the hope that they will be pacified and not wreak vengeance on the innocent."[14] The *segaki-kuyoo*, therefore, conveyed a recognition of one's closeness to

death, and what death can mean, depending on one's connectedness or disconnectedness to a household: benign existence as an
ancestral spirit or tormented existence between life and death as a
muenbotoke (wandering spirit).

The *segaki-kuyoo* that I witnessed struck me as a rather odd event,
a juxtaposition of emotional depth and levity. Parishioners began
arriving early, crowding into the temple, then spilling out the open
doorways onto a large veranda, all of them wearing somber colors,
black, gray, deep purple. The nervous flicking of the women's
small, scented fans only made the heat and humidity more unbearable, for they filled the air with a sickly sweet smell of san-
dalwood. Suddenly, there was a sharp ringing of chimes, and a
long procession of priests elaborately costumed in gold, crimson,
black, and crisp white began to cut through the crowd.

While the head priest and his disciples circled the altar, ringing
bells and chanting sutras, the parishioners fell into a soft chatter,
largely ignoring the activities around the gilded Buddha. The men
and women around me leaned over to complain about the heat,
gossip about who had recently gotten married, and how they were
related to the newly deceased. Children were released from their
seats and wandered about aimlessly. The emotional tenor changed
quite dramatically as the priests began chanting the names of those
who had died within the last year: men cried softly; women sobbed;
and the children stared, awestruck. This quiet show of sadness
subsided as a queue formed to light incense, the final act of
purification.

After about an hour and a half, the priest and the last disciple
filed out, and the mass came to a close with a rapid, high-pitched
beating of drums and wooden clappers, reminiscent of the end of
Kabuki dramas. The crowd immediately dispersed, dashing about,
almost shoving one another in the hurry to gather up *otooba* (memorial slats),[15] which they then placed on family tombs in the temple
graveyard. The slow, heavy atmosphere of the *segaki-kuyoo* gave
way to laughter, as everyone scrambled to get home to prepare for
the return of their ancestors on July 13. The parishioners had only
three days left in which to clean their houses, set up the special
obon altars, and prepare for the visit of the priest, who would

perform a private mass for the household dead with all members of the *ie* present.

"For the Japanese family," wrote Ooms, "the *o-bon* is the highlight of the year. During these days, each house becomes its own temple so to speak: a temporary sacred place, the altar is built where 'the sacred' will stay during the time of *o-bon*. The members of the household themselves perform the rites."[16] Household members *alone* are responsible for maintaining the realm of the sacred: members set up the altars, make offerings of food and prayer, secure the presence of a priest to chant sutras. Members of the household not only maintain but create the sacred. In fact, they are active participants in creating ancestors-cum-gods.

During one of those days of *obon*, I followed Hasegawa-sensei as he paid calls on several households. Because he was the head priest, he visited only the important patrons of his temple. He explained to me that the *obon* altars that I was about to see were very elaborate versions of those found in more "simple" homes: his temple's patrons had the time and money to maintain the traditions of the past. The altars took the general form shown in Figure 5.

When I asked what all of the various plants signified, no one was quite sure. They just "did it," year after year. Hasegawa-sensei told me that if I *really* wanted to know, he would introduce me to folklorists. About the incense, however, they were sure that it was for *okiyome* (purification), just as the water in the lotus-leaf bowl was sprinkled with the bush clover on the 108 pieces of eggplant to cleanse life of the 108 sins of humankind. The *okusama* giggled when the household head explained to me that the cucumber with four toothpicks stuck in it was a horse, just as the eggplant was an ox: they provided a mode of transportation for their ancestors on their long journey from, and back to, the spirit world.

Although the household head and the *okusama* were obviously proud of the *obon* altar, they denigrated it by complaining about how all the objects seemed to be old and dirty, especially the miniature trays, chopsticks, and utensils set on the floor. I knew that the food offerings on level 2 of the altar were for the household ancestors, but the little trays on the floor were puzzling.

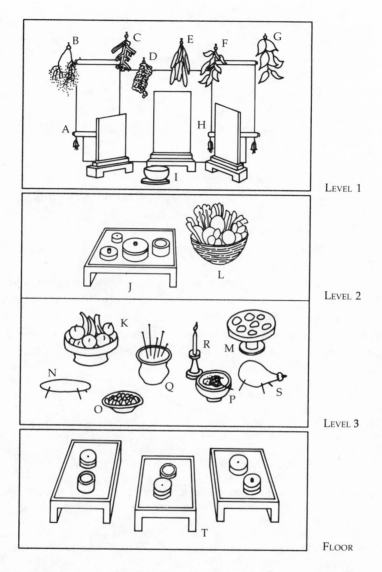

LEVEL 1

LEVEL 2

LEVEL 3

FLOOR

Figure 5. The *Obon* altar. Objects include: A, commemorative scrolls purchased by members of the household on pilgrimages; B, *awa* (millet); C, *sugi* (Japanese cedar); D, *hagi* (bush clover); E, *gama* (cattail); F, *hoozuki* (ground cherry); G, *kuri no ha* (chestnut leaves); H, *ihai* (ancestral tablets); I, a cup of tea; J, a tray of *osonae mono* (offerings of cooked food); K, a dish of fruit; L, a wicker basket of fresh vegetables; M, a dish of *dango* (dumplings); N, a cucumber "horse"; O, a dish with 108 pieces of eggplant on a lotus leaf; P, a bowl of water with a lotus leaf and bush clover; Q, a container for lighting incense; R, a lighted candle; S, an eggplant "ox"; and T, a set of miniature trays for *osonae mono*.

73

"What are they?" I asked the *okusama*.

"They're for the wandering spirits."

"Who are the *muenbotoke*?"

"Oh, they're the unfilial."

"Who are the unfilial?"

"Those who died as children, or those who died before marriage."

"Do you have *ihai* for them?"

"No. But we feel sorry for them, and so we should feed them too. That's what the little trays are for."

The *okusama* added that the tatami for level 3 of the altar was changed every year, and the old mat was given to the wandering spirits to use under their trays on the floor.

The concept of *muenbotoke* is fascinating for it provides a foil for the ancestors, which defines by contrast who the ancestors are. Not everyone is elected to ancestorhood at death. Clearly, in the case of the household that I visited during *obon*, children and the unmarried were excluded. David Plath wrote about the *muenbotoke* as "outsiders":

> The outsiders form a residual category. They are at the fringes of institutionalization, where conditions of membership are not easy to state with precision. They include all homeless souls who are not regularly affiliated with any household line, or whose line has lapsed. But they also may include the souls of dead guests, probationary members, etc., who remain nearby but who eventually should return to join the departed in their own household.
>
> Outsiders are not usually admitted to the household shelf [*but-sudan*]. Some families provide a separate shelf for them, outside the house or on a veranda. Usually this is a temporary shelf, erected only on a few ceremonial occasions during the year. The household shelf, by contrast, is permanent. Nor is there ordinarily a household tablet [*ihai*] for the outsiders, although communities sometimes collectively honor their unknown dead. Retirement is undefined, and about all that can be said of tenure is that the outsiders are generally suspect. Presumably they are quite unhappy over their situation . . . and they deserve at least an occasional charitable nod.[17]

There are several ways in which one could be condemned to the status of wandering spirit, to the residual category of outsider: by dying a violent death, by committing suicide, by allowing the household line to die out, or by dying as a child or as an unmarried adult. All ways are equally abhorrent. In the case of the household line dying out, the soul of the dead has been *dis*connected from an *ie*. In the case of the child or unmarried adult in death, the soul is still *un*connected to an *ie*.[18] In fact, Ooms remarked that in the latter case "it seems that the status of *muenbotoke* is unchangeable and intrinsically linked with the position they had, while still alive in the *ie*: they are souls of those members who are unable to join some line of ancestors or to start their own. From the moment of their death, these souls cannot change their position within the *ie*. If at this time they were still members of their family of orientation and had never established their family of procreation, they are condemned to become *muenbotoke*."[19] If one, therefore, fails to obtain a position of permanent membership in an *ie*, one is condemned to wander about, tormented in death. Because there are only two permanent positions, household head and household wife, the path to ancestorhood is rather restricted, as shown in Figure 6. Since the ultimate attainment of ancestorhood is determined by the attainment of a permanent position in an extant household, and since the attainment of ancestorhood does not occur automatically but depends on the observation of seasonal, yearly, monthly, and daily rites of worship by the living in the *ie*, every *ie* is a temple, not only during *obon* but every day. The mundane is securely tied to the otherworldly, the sacred. It was in this context that David Plath observed that in Japan the family of God is the family.[20]

Death and History

The rites performed by members of the *ie* to facilitate status transitions in the realm of the dead, from *shiryoo* to *senzo*, may be classified into two categories: the personal and the ancestral. Although the personal and the ancestral often overlap, seasonal rites tend to be weighted toward the ancestral, and the yearly, monthly, and daily rites toward the personal. The *segaki-kuyoo* that I witnessed was a combination of the personal and the ancestral. Al-

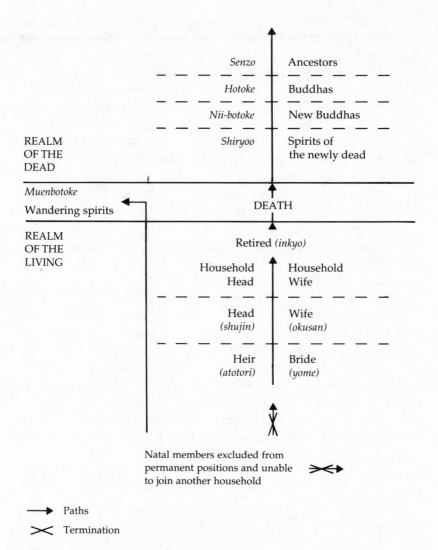

Figure 6. Paths for the living and the dead. I have borrowed from two figures, one drawn by David W. Plath and the other by Robert J. Smith. Plath, "Where the Family of God Is the Family," *American Anthropologist*, 66 (1964), 305; Smith, *Ancestor Worship in Contemporary Japan* (Stanford University Press, 1974), 57.

though the collectivity of ancestral spirits was worshiped, the recently deceased were given special attention, for this first *obon* was especially important in their personal cycle of attaining ancestorhood. Subsequent *obon* would be less important in the personal cycle. As the deceased makes his or her way into ancestorhood, the personal rites take on less significance and the ancestral rites, which are seasonal, take on greater significance.

The personal rites are keyed to the date of death and subsequent commemorative anniversaries, which are periodic (*nenki*), annual (*sho-tsuki-meinichi*), and monthly (*mai-tsuki-meinichi*). Personal rites are tied to the specifics of the deceased, and as these specifics are gradually forgotten (including the date of his or her death), ancestral rites become the only way to venerate the dead. As the personal moves into the realm of the collective ancestral, periods of worship move from specific deathdays to the seasonal, in which *all* the dead participate. Thus, in the personal cycle, the important dates are the forty-ninth day after death, the hundredth day, the first year, the third year, the seventh year, the thirteenth year, the twenty-third, and the final thirty-third or fiftieth anniversary of death. The seasonal rites are observed during the equinoxes and *obon*. Although the equinoxes (*ohigan*) and *obon* are celebrated in the personal cycle, for the deceased is part of the collective dead, the most important seasonal rite is the first *obon* after death, when the *nii-botoke* (the new buddha) is sent away with the other dead and becomes a *hotoke* (buddha); at this point, the deceased is clearly on his or her way to ancestorhood. At the *tomurai-age* (last of the periodic deathday anniversaries), the *hotoke* becomes a *senzo* (ancestor). At this thirty-third anniversary of death, the *ihai* is taken from the household ancestral altar and deposited at the temple.[21] Its replacement is already in the ancestral altar in the form of an *ie senzodaidai ihai*, a memorial tablet for the "generations upon generations of ancestors." The households with which I was familiar took the *ihai* to the temple and replaced them with *kuri-ihai*, which are especially thin wooden tablets that are stacked together like a deck of cards and put into a container. No one could remember who those ancestors were, although their posthumous names were inscribed on the *kuri-ihai*. Hasegawa-sensei told me that very often

77

no one did anything with the *ihai* after the *tomurai-age*: it was simply pushed to the back of the *butsudan*, and after a certain amount of crowding in the ancestral altar, someone might take it upon himself or herself to bring the *ihai* to the temple.

Although the thirty-third anniversary of death may be considered the official transition point into ancestorhood, no one is quite sure when, exactly, the *hotoke* becomes a *senzo*. It could occur years before or after that date. It simply depends on the process of forgetting. As Plath observed: "The ancestors are all the departed regular members of a household who have been expunged from living memory." When the departed members of the household are expunged from memory, "the soul melts into the household 'choir invisible,' an everlasting and unnumbered plurality."[22] Thus, living members of an *ie* are given both a right and a rather carefully structured way to forget their dead. From the departed's point of view, to be carefully forgotten is to be allowed the path to a sacred existence as an ancestor. Once joined with the "choir invisible," the departed becomes the object of ancestral veneration. Hasegawa-sensei explained to me that the ancestors are not merely "There." They are part of life, part of a life movement, much like the evolving of one season into another. Hasegawa-sensei, however, was quick to point out that this movement is not cyclical but progressive. Take, for example, *ohigan*, the spring and autumn equinoxes that mark important periods of ancestor worship. The equinoxes also mark time as the movement of life through the seasons. *Ohigan* is written *ka no kishi* (the far shore). The far shore symbolizes life's purpose, but once having reached that shore, one discovers that there are endless more shores. During *ohigan* one goes to the household tomb and pays respect to the ancestors; one makes an earnest pledge in front of the ancestors about one's purpose in life. The steady marking of time by the seasons holds one responsible for having done some positive good for the *ie*. Each extant generation feels the full weight of its household's history, as Smith wrote:

> The Japanese believe that the actions and initiatives of the living determine the outcome of efforts to improve one's lot in this world. The ancestors are . . . felt to enjoy a generally passive existence, over-

seeing the actions of the living in the manner of tutelary deities. Thus, the living bear a heavy burden with respect to the household dead. The spirits of the ancestors are felt to be overjoyed at any positive achievement by a descendant, and are indeed given some of the credit for success, but *the full onus of failure falls on the living alone.*[23]

David Plath translated an amusing passage from a popular sociology text entitled *Me and You: Modern Family Life and Views*:

You probably all have had the experience of having graduated from school and gotten a job, and when you received your first pay your mother took the pay envelope, displayed it on the household shelf [*butsudan*], and offered a candle. This probably is a survival of rites to indicate that you have come of age and been added as one link in the social bonds of the household as a unit.

Or a more extreme situation is when we often are dragged by Dad or Mom to the front of the household shelf and asked "Do you think you can give any excuse to the ancestors for doing that?" The shelf is associated with the household and society, so that rebelling before it is like rebelling against the whole world; and this is why a lecture in front of the shelf has such potency.[24]

Held accountable to the spirits of household ancestors, the living are responsible for historical progress in the household line, at least, and, perhaps, for historical progress in Japanese society itself.

The historical presence of ancestors comes from the distant past. It is completely different from the historical presence of *hotokesama*, whose presence is one of the near past. They are still alive in the memories of the living. Until the departed fade completely into the realm of the dead and become ancestors, they are treated as though they were alive, quite literally, in the performance of personal rites. Robert J. Smith told a wonderful story of an American couple who were invited to a memorial service given by a widow for her late husband. Everything was completely traditional, except for a chocolate cake, which she had baked especially for the occasion. It bore the frosted inscription, "Happy Anniversary Mr. Y———." Chocolate cake was one of her late husband's favorite foods. "It is scarcely necessary to remark," wrote Smith, "that as the individual fades in the memory of his family such personal touches are abandoned, first because no one remembers his or her tastes very clearly, and second because with the passage of time his spirit is thought to have become in some degree purified and no longer very attached to the world he knew. But until this fading occurs, the spirit of the dead is liable to be dealt with in a very literal way, as though he were still alive."[25]

The intimate quality of the personal rites reveals the lingering attachment of the dead to the living, or more appropriately, the living to the dead. This kind of attachment can be seen in the fact that copies of *ihai* are made. For example, a daughter who has married may ask permission from the household head of her natal family to allow her to make copies of her deceased parents' *ihai*. She will place these copies in the *butsudan* of her new household, where she can venerate her deceased parents and thereby receive emotional comfort. As the days, months, and years pass after the day of death, the living slowly let go of the dead, and the dead begin to play a less significant role in the lives of the living. But until that happens, the dead and their *ihai* do more than simply provide comfort for the living while they adjust to life without their loved ones.

When Makoto Moriuchi received his letter of acceptance from Princeton University, he told his mother the good news, and they both immediately headed for the cabinet that served as the *butsudan* for Mr. Moriuchi's *ihai* and photo. Opening the cabinet doors with a bang, forgoing the ritual of lighting votive candles to "call him back," Makoto presented his letter of acceptance, translated it for his father, and thanked him for all his help. Mrs. Moriuchi told her husband that this proved to the world, and especially to Uncle Masao, that he wasn't such a stupid man after all, for his son could actually attend an elite American university. Both Makoto and his mother were in tears.

Later that night, after their evening baths, Makoto, Nobuko, and Akiko piled onto their mother's bed, as they were wont to do whenever they sought solace or good conversation. It was a sad moment for them. Makoto's success only reminded them of Mr. Moriuchi, who had died a disappointed man. He never made it to the position of household head, and thus he didn't have the necessary social, economic, and political influence to realize his dreams. Mr. Moriuchi wanted to "open up" Japanese society, make Japan more *kokusaiteki* (international). Yet he spoke poor English and Italian. The house that he commissioned and in which the Moriuchis lived was to reflect his cosmopolitan tastes. It turned out to be a large, rambling collection of cylinders and cubes, glass bricks, concrete walls, hardwood floors, and oddly intrusive Japanese gardens. All in all, it was a poor example of Japan's early postmodern sensibility.

Mr. Moriuchi wanted Japan to be less "rigid," as he saw it. He had great visions, yet they seemed extremely narrow, for he could not see beyond his *ie*. He sought alternatives, yet saw none.

Makoto was surprised to find himself the next morning at the edge of his mother's bed. He had drifted off into a deep sleep, thinking about his father. He got up resolved to do in his life what his father had not been able to accomplish. It was the only way he knew how, or was able, to return to his father all the love, kindness, and nurturance he had received. Although Mr. Moriuchi was trapped in the feuds of the *ie*, trapped in the often rigidly defined lifestyle of elite households in Japanese society, he paved the way for an alternative path for his children: an education at the American School in Japan; summer camps in the Poconos and Lausanne; lessons in English, French, and German. He refused to buy his daughters kimono, saying that they were not merely Japanese but "international," that they would have an alternative to "good marriages." Nobuko and Akiko were to wear American jeans, seek careers, and change Japan. Makoto, the sensitive soul, was designated the writer, the poet. When he recounted to me his moment of insight into his future course, he said, "Kokoro no naka ni kakugo shita." By using the word *kakugo* to express his feelings of resolve, Makoto made it very clear that he had no other alternative but to carry out his father's wishes in his life, for *kakugo* means to be *resigned* to one's circumstances, as well as to be *determined* to act. "Deep in my heart, I became resolved."

Makoto's attachment to his deceased father, an example of a general phenomenon, was not a morbid attachment. The living are not stuck in the past, in life as it used to be when the *hotokesama* was still a living member of the household. In fact, this attachment allows the living to act on the world, for it clearly helps them define goals and objectives. The presence of the household *hotokesama*, unlike the presence of the household ancestors, comes from the immediate past, with immediate consequences. Whereas the presence of ancestors compels the living through a general sense of moral and ethical responsibility to act in a manner that is both good and progressive, the immediate past in the presence of *hotokesama* defines what is good and progressive in the temporal present. In a sense, the dead participate in the household by helping define the goals of the living. The dead, and the rites that involve them, take the living from the past to the present and allow them to anticipate the future. Death in the household, therefore, not only is history but makes history.

Belief and Disbelief: Death and Its Transcendence

"You still talk to your father, don't you, Makoto?" I asked.
"Yes, we all do."
"So you think he's still around?"
"I told you before that just because he died, it doesn't mean that he doesn't exist."
"So he's still here."
"Probably."
"Do you *really* believe that he's still in the house, at this very moment?"
"I don't know."
"Well, do you or don't you believe it?"
"Kankei nai daroo" (It really doesn't matter, does it?). The reply was curt. Makoto's irritation was clear, and I backed off.

The same question that bothered me also bothered Herman Ooms. Ooms asked his informants if the ancestors lived on in some form or another, in some place, "here" or "there." A sixty-seven-year-old head of a main family replied that "he lived constantly in their [the ancestor's] presence. This same informant told us also that, every year at *o-bon*, he held the welcome fire as soon as possible in order that the ancestors may stay longer. (Four months later at *o-bon*, when we checked this, it proved indeed to be true: he was at least two hours ahead of his neighbours for the welcome fire.)." Another informant, a woman of sixty-three, expressed restrained belief in the presence of ancestors at commemorative rites: "They might come or not come, but in any case, I feel as if they were here."[26]

Ooms's informants also exhibited sheer skepticism. For example, a women of thirty-three said, "All this talk about ancestors protecting us are but nice lies." Yet this same woman said that she would continue the performance of ancestral rites: "It is a bother and does not have any special meaning, but I probably will make the offerings. Doesn't one do these things naturally?" A seventy-year-old woman, who did not believe that *tatari* were a real threat nor that one was obligated to perform the rites, said, "My mind is not at peace when I do not make the offerings." A man of forty-five remarked, "We are deeply bound by custom; the meaning escapes us and neither good nor bad results follow from the veneration or neglect of the ancestors."[27]

This question of belief or disbelief in the existence of ancestors was extremely important to me. It didn't make sense to me that my informants continued to carry out the personal and ancestral rites of death, albeit with varying degrees of conviction, if they did not *know* whether the dead continued to exist and whether the dead had a real effect on their lives. After they performed some rite pertaining to death and ancestorhood, I would collar my informants and ask, "Do you really believe that the dead still continue to exist, that they are around somewhere?" Invariably, the answers would be to the effect: "Gee, I wonder." Or, "I don't know." Makoto Moriuchi's irritable reply, however, seemed right on target: "It really doesn't matter, does it?"

Makoto was absolutely right. I was barking up the wrong tree. My questions about belief or disbelief were based on standards of objective knowledge that have little to do with subjective reality, ritual experience. By asking whether my informants believed that the dead were really "around" *after* the ritual experience had occurred, I was subjecting them to an unfair question: Can you prove it? Of course not. After having left the realm of ritual reality, informants moved into the realm of stark objectivity, where facts are prone to scientific verification: Show me that it's true. Since none of my informants could prove, for sure, that the dead were still around, not one of them could claim unqalified belief. However, just because they could not claim belief under my scientifically oriented interrogation, it does not necessarily follow that they did not believe in the presence of the dead in the realm of the ritual. In terms of modes of understanding, there is a significant difference between the cognitive/objective and the emotive/subjective, between the mundane and the ritual. What is felt to be true in ritual experience may not correspond to what is thought to be true in mundane experience. But the point is: one form of understanding does not negate the other. For example, when Makoto Moriuchi opened his family's *butsudan* and introduced me to his deceased father, even I participated in the ritual experience by bowing and saying, "Nice to meet you." I felt Mr. Moriuchi's presence. When Makoto snickered, I was brought back from the ritual to the mundane and *thought* that Mr. Moriuchi's presence couldn't be real. Did I or didn't I believe? I don't know.

What is thought does not completely override what is felt. Both are essential. Hasegawa-sensei made this point when he told me that the understanding of death's relationship to life, of one's past to one's present, of history, does not come from the intellect, but from the heart. And this kind of understanding can only come through repeated ritual experience, where things are felt rather than known. He said, "Unless people feel deeply, all is for naught." And what is deeply felt is the presence of the dead.

Although there is a difference between the cognitive/objective and the emotive/subjective, between the mundane and the ritual, we must not consider that difference to be a gap. Both modes of understanding exist as the recto and verso on the plane of everyday experience. For example, the felt presence of the dead in ancestral rites informs mundane behavior by imparting a general sense of moral and ethical responsibility to the living, leading them to act in a positive manner, to contribute to the progressive history of the household. The felt presence of the dead in the personal rites of death informs the mundane by helping the living define what it means to act in a positive manner.[28] Ancestors and *hotokesama* are forms of history, from the distant and near past, forms that combine in the feeling of *kakugo*, a deep sense of *determination* to act upon the world, as well as a sense of *resignation* to act upon the world in a certain, predetermined way. The presence of history, indeed, the force of history, is inescapable, just as death is inescapable. Thus, through ritual experience, men and women of the *ie* retrospectively order the past so that the present can be understood and the future anticipated. The past, therefore, is structured as prologue through death and its transcendence in the household: the understanding of death allows the living to act upon the world.

5 AUTHORITY

The anthropologist Chie Nakane warned that in the apparently cohesive structure of the *ie* there exists slightly below the surface the possibility of open conflict. What gives the *ie* its strength, that is, centralized control through a corporate and hierarchical structure, is the source of its potential demise. Figure 7 illustrates this point.

The basic structure of the *ie* is a set of paired, vertical relationships that is simply multiplied. In the *doozoku gaisha*, *A* represents not only the main family but also the main enterprise, *B* a branch family and subsidiary, and *D* a subbranch family and a subsidiary of a subsidiary. The relationship between *A* and *D* operates through *B*, just as the relationship between *B* and *C* operates through *A*. The horizontal relationship between *B* and *C* is much less important than the vertical relationships *A-B* and *A-C*.

Figure 7 represents a "lineage," a set of relationships within a compound household, which has little to do with rendering biogenetic relationships understandable and a lot to do with securing power and mobilizing resources.[1] Keith Brown pressed this point further by analyzing *doozoku* (compound household) relationships over generational changes (Fig. 8).

A is the head of the main family of the entire *ie*, represented over five generations. The relationship between main family head *A* and branch family head *B*, whose family had branched four

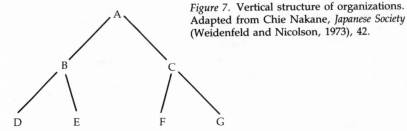

Figure 7. Vertical structure of organizations. Adapted from Chie Nakane, *Japanese Society* (Weidenfeld and Nicolson, 1973), 42.

generations ago, would be just as significant as that between *A* and *C*, whose family had branched only one generation ago. To further reinforce the notion that the *ie* is primarily based on corporate rather than biogenetic relationships, Brown noted that although main family head *A* may be a first cousin of subbranch family head *F* and only a distant cousin of branch family head *B*, the tie between *A* and *B* is closer than the tie between *A* and *F*. In spite of the geneological distance between *A* and *B*, their main/branch relationship is considered more significant than the main/subbranch relationship of *A* and *F*.[2]

This lineage orders relationships within the *ie* so that groups relate to one another as subordinates and superiors. In Figure 7, for main family head *A* to exact a service from subbranch family head *D*, he must operate through *B*. Lineage orders relationships of reciprocity as well as power. Thus, in order for subbranch family head *D* to ask main family head *A* to make accessible communal resources or capital goods not otherwise available to the subbranch, he must operate through *B*. Through this lineage, the *ie* can easily expand to meet the demands of an ever-increasing amount of human and material resources, while still maintaining centralized control. We find concepts such as *kei* (descent) abstracted out of the biogenetic reality of procreation and employed to order social relationships that prove highly adaptable to economic pursuits. The family is not the enterprise. Family and enterprise simply share a common social template.

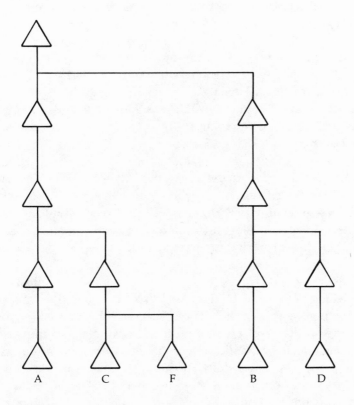

Figure 8. Structure of the *Doozoku*. Adapted from Keith Brown, "The Content of *Doozoku* Relationships in Japan," *Ethnology*, 7:2 (1968), 118.

In Figure 7, direct ties between *B* and *C* are weak or virtually nonexistent. What would happen should leader *A* be removed? Nakane noted that "in a group structure of this nature a change of leadership leads to a very critical period for the continuance and stability of the group. In many cases groups split into a number of small and hostile segments after the death of the leader."[3]

Given the vertical and corporate structure of group life, relationships of power and dependence are necessarily asymmetric. The point that Nakane makes, however, is that the asymmetry is not necessarily accepted. As Nakane bluntly stated, "A system based on vertical relationships works effectively when the junior member is content with his position under his senior."[4] The death of a leader triggers the process of succession, which, in essence, puts to test the acceptance of this asymmetry in relationships of power. For the successor, such acceptance means that power may be exercised legitimately, that is, with authority. Should he not be granted the grace of legitimacy, power becomes merely coercive, breeding dissent and the eventual destruction of the corporate group.

Legitimacy rests on the concept of lineage as it manifests itself in the history of the *ie*, linking the present household with its past, connecting the present household head with past occupants of his esteemed office. We saw that on the familial plane of the *ie*, strict adherence to the biological requirements of patrilineal descent is routinely ignored in order that the most able available man can serve as leader of the household in a perpetual social group. Yet, if asked about his lineage, any household head would turn to the household altar, point to the ancestral tablets, and claim that the crowd composes his direct ascendants. Adopted sons, or adopted married couples, brought in as successors a few generations back are conveniently forgotten. Again, the concept of descent has little or nothing to do with geneological relationships. Rather, it serves as an ideology that orders the history of the *ie*. As such, the ideology of patrilineal descent is a testament to the service of men for the sake of the perpetual household. To occupy the office of household head and to exercise power from that position means, therefore, that one is acting not out of personal interest but in the name of a compulsory institution, the *ie*. One acts in the name of a higher order, thus sparing the exercise of power the nakedness of coercion and granting it the grace of authority. In this sense, patrilineal descent may not be real in biological terms, but it is real in the realm of the symbolic and the emotive, ordering the history of a household so that the cultural ideal of individual sacrifices for the corporate group becomes an inherent aspect of leadership. The very existence of yet another generation to continue the "line of descent," the "patrilineage," attests to the strength of that ideal.

Tales of Sacrifice

At 6:30 in the morning, on an unbearably bright Thursday in March 1981, the telephone rang. It was Makoto Moriuchi: "Matt, get up, and get the first train possible to Misaki. I'll meet you there. Oh, and don't forget your swimsuit."

I arrived, groggy, unshaven, and irritated at Makoto's irrepressibly cheery self. My mood deteriorated further as we climbed into a bus crammed with housewives on the way home from their morning shopping. After forty-five tortuous minutes of winding down a country road to the sea coast, we stepped off the bus, and I, reeling with motion sickness, stepped into a pothole, falling against a rotted bamboo fence. Makoto said, "Isn't it beautiful?"

"What is?"

It was breathtaking: a grand little house with a thatched roof, perched high on a cliff above a sun-drenched cove. Like children engaged in some deliciously evil act, we sneaked around the house, found a loose storm window, and entered.

As I was changing into my Speedo in the formal tea ceremony room, a toothless, extraordinarily wrinkled face appeared at the open window, shouting, "Makoto! Makoto!" Petrified, I waited for Makoto, who strolled by me, muttering, "What a bother."

It was the caretaker. He told Makoto, as he had done countless times before, that it would have been easier for Makoto to get the key from him than to climb through windows and break locks.

Makoto lied, promising not to do this again. The old man smiled his toothless smile, bowed respectfully, and informed us that he was going to call Makoto's mother to let her know that we were at the Misaki beachhouse. Before leaving, he asked, "And what's *his* name?" We were going to be told on. The game had been spoiled.

My friendship with Makoto was based on a need to break rules. (We also shared an undisciplined love of literature of the American South and a devotion to Iris Murdoch's noels. He found me a more than willing companion in his odd pastime: sneaking by caretakers to peer into, or actually break into, the vacation homes and the various residences of the Moriuchi household. And it was the same whenever we got caught. We would immediately fall into a sad, dispirited state. It was not different on this particular day.

The sea was a cobalt blue and still wintry. Fishermen's wives were gathering and drying seaweed for the local market. Makoto and I collected shells on the beach, swam, ate sashimi, and read, huddled under blankets in the sun, completely mute. As the evening approached, we headed indoors to pull open drawers, dig through boxes, and to try on the funny clothing that years of guests had left behind, the source of inspiration for the many plays that he, Nobuko, and Akiko had years earlier mounted for Mom and Dad. Makoto walked in on me and my little fantasy, just as I was completing my costume: a floppy hat left behind by an American matron in the fifties to go with a pair of striped *monpe*, knickers that the local fishmongers prefer. He showed me a book.

"What's that?"

"Required reading. Everyone in our household has had to read this."

I listened to the opening: "The world around our household completely collapsed. The old feudal estates were abolished at the turn of the century. Not only was our income eliminated but so was our standing in society. If it were not for the Meiji Government, I would have been lord of the province."

It was the voice of Makoto's grandfather, speaking through him, recounting the battles won and lost by the men of the Moriuchi household since the *ie*'s founding in the fifteenth century.

He continued: "My father had to seek work so that we could eat. He gave up the way of the warrior and founded a small manufacturing company."

"I am now devoted to that company. Moriuchi Industries is my castle. By building Moriuchi Industries, I am building Japanese society."

"Families are frightening," Makoto said, tossing the small book aside. This was the beginning of a quiet evening in which I became engrossed in Makoto's stories about his grandfather and his family. As we brewed some tea, Makoto admitted that it was fear that motivated his deep curiosity about his household; fear drew him into the various houses and compounds, to peer and investigate, in a desperate attempt to understand the strange power of his family, a power that seemed inescapable. This dark, voyeuristic curiosity began in his early childhood, when Grandfather would summon all of his children and grandchildren to the main house in Tokyo for family events.

Grandfather never seemed to remember any of his grandchildren's names but would call out, waving his right arm in a slow arc, "Grandchildren, all of you, come here." With his dark kimono, shock of white hair, and sunken eyes, he was a terrifying presence, sitting at the edge of a large room that opened on to the garden. When they gathered about him, he actually said nothing, except: "That kid's Makoto, right?"

He remembered only Makoto's name. Struck dumb in his presence, Makoto would fix his eyes on his grandfather, and both would fall into a silent staring. It was only recently, when Makoto turned twenty, that his mother explained the strange phenomenon to him. Makoto, apparently, resembled his deceased grandmother. Grandmother was not typical of the women in the Moriuchi household. In other words, she was far from elegant: her mouth was too large; her nose was too sharply defined; her eyes were a bit off-center; and she was tall to the point of being gawky—quite clumsy from what everyone says. Yet her memory lives on with the greatest

93

respect, for as Makoto's mother made clear, the entire Moriuchi household has basked in the good graces of society because of Grandmother's work.

Grandmother was an immensely generous woman, but her open hand tended to irritate her children, for whatever seemed of value to them, she gave away, from cakes to love. It was said that she took better care of strangers than of her own children, children who resented the fact that they were each assigned an *uba* (wet nurse) who tended to their needs and disciplining.

Makoto's mother explained, however, that Grandmother could not help putting the care of her children in others' hands, for she played such an important role in getting Moriuchi Industries off the ground. Grandmother was always present in the shadows, keeping an eye on Grandfather, for he was a tyrant, ill-tempered and shrewd, stepping on a lot of sensitive feelings. She would be the one to say goodbye at the door, pressing money and goodwill on those he might have offended. Grandmother's actions were perfect examples of *naijo no koo* (good works of a wife). She repaired any of the relationships that might have been damaged by her husband's obstinacy. She understood people and how they related to each other. She knew how to evaluate and analyze social situations. She kept the *ningen kankei* (human relationships) going.

Makoto never knew his grandmother, but he and his sisters lived with her legend. Grandmother was perfect; Grandmother was generous; Grandmother might not have been a beauty, but she was loved and respected; Grandmother suffered tremendously, and that is what made her the ideal person. Grandmother was *kazoku no giseisha*, a family martyr. "But," Makoto asserted, "I refuse to become another *giseisha*."

In that statement, Makoto denied one of the basic principles of life espoused by his grandfather, who wrote: "I know that with the postwar reforms toward democracy, it is unfashionable to praise the ways of our past. But it cannot be denied that our feudal heritage has made us what we are today. The values that made one yield one's full allegiance to one's lord and that made one offer one's unmitigated devotion to one's parents are at the very core of our current economic success. Loyalty, devotion, and service are part of the spirit of feudal society, a society built on complete self-sacrifice. This spirit is behind every successful undertaking in modern Japanese society."

The continuance of the Moriuchi household for almost five hundred years of Japanese history, according to Grandfather, is directly attributed to the sacrifice of the personal for the collective, of the individual for the sake of the institution. In the pamphlet that he wrote especially for his family, he carefully documented the individual contributions of men toward the development of the *ie*, yet the sacrifices of women, even those of his own wife, go unmentioned. That task is left to women, as they hand down their version of household history in tales told by mothers to children.

Grandmother, according to Makoto's mother, came to the Moriuchi's great house in southern Japan at the age of twelve or thirteen. She accompanied her mother, who was employed as a household servant. Although both mother and daughter wore crested kimono, they were not of samurai background but were from a high merchant household that had fallen on hard times. Servitude had become their lot in life. No one could understand why Grandfather insisted on marrying her, but he did. The Moriuchi household asked another illustrious *ie* to adopt Grandmother, thereby permitting the marriage between her and Grandfather. Thus, through adoption, she became an *ojoosama* (young lady). After attaining that position, she became qualified for yet another: the *oyome-san* (young bride) of the *atotori* (designated successor) of the Moriuchi household.

Makoto asked his mother if Grandfather married Grandmother out of love, and Mrs. Moriuchi simply said, "No."

"Was it out of a sense of charity?"

"No."

"What was it, then?"

"It was an obsession." An obsession that is yet to be understood by anyone.

Grandmother had a strange hold on Grandfather. He resented her, yet found his life to be inseparable from hers. Grandfather's hidden despair was never expressed in any direct way to Grandmother. Instead, his angst transformed into a dislike of his eldest son, the *choonan* of the Moriuchi household and Grandmother's favorite child.

While Grandfather tried to deny the very existence of the *choonan*, Grandmother denied him nothing. She loved the *choonan*, Tetsuo, deeply, looked after his interests, protected him from Grandfather's vengeance, spoiled him. While all the other children were given to wet nurses, she coddled him and personally looked after his every need. This child represented her power, as well as the dependence of Grandfather and almost five hundred years of Moriuchi history on that power. Her son would be the next head of the household.

In 1955, Grandmother died at the age of fifty-six, just after seeing her beloved Tetsuo installed as president of the newly established Moriuchi Industrial Design and Construction, a *kogaisha* (subsidiary) of Moriuchi Industries. It was a coup for Grandmother, for although she had been able to convince Grandfather to give Tetsuo a titular position and an income as a member of the board of directors of the main enterprise, only the presidency of an important subsidiary would give Tetsuo power, that is, the ability to move both human and material resources. At the age of forty, Tetsuo was finally separated from his mother's guidance and protection. He was left to face the future and his father, alone.

Struggles and Strategies

In later conversations with Makoto I learned that Grandfather was not at all displeased with the decision to place Tetsuo in the presidency of a subsidiary, for it was a routine procedure, carried out according to the organizational principles of branching. Moriuchi Industries had been growing at a rapid pace, moving to dominate a particular sector of the Japanese economy. The *oyagaisha* (main enterprise) would be the manufacturing base, and Moriuchi Industrial Design and Construction would use that base to move into plant construction—a simple strategy of forward integration within one sector of the economy. Later, as high technology became an increasingly important aspect of Moriuchi Industries' products,

Moriuchi Science and Technology was established, with the third son, Tasaburo (Makoto's father), at its head. Then, Moriuchi Properties, with the fourth son, Haruo, as the head, was established to handle the real estate involved in plant sites. Helping Tetsuo establish a *kogaisha* made rational-economic sense to Grandfather as head of the enterprise; an expanding industry needed an expanding corporate structure. As head of the household, it also made sense to him to establish a *bunke* (branch family). Setting up a *bunke* clearly meant that Tetsuo was being placed outside the *honke* (main family).

This "lineage" should have been formed and maintained by mutual agreement, continuing as long as it was economically and socially viable.[5] As Ezra Vogel pointed out, "in business families the selection of someone other than first sons as successors was based primarily on competence and that the setting up of branch families to be related to the main families was often done in this context."[6] In this particular case, competence was not the primary issue. Rather, sentiments were behind the organizational developments.

Grandfather's move to establish a subsidiary with Tetsuo at its head was interpreted quite differently by Grandmother. She did not see it as a way of shutting Tetsuo out of the *honke*. Instead, she saw it as a way for him eventually to attain the headship of the main family as well as the presidency of Moriuchi Industries, the main enterprise. Grandmother latched on to the issue of competency, interpreting the establishment of a subsidiary as a chance for Tetsuo to prove himself worthy of moving back into the main family and enterprise. For Grandmother, it was a rational-economic move that was publicly visible, a move that she hoped would overcome Grandfather's irrational feelings. Merit, she believed, would overcome personal sentiments.

Two drastically different interpretations of a situation were possible because of the uncertainty created by not following the rules of branching exactly. In other words, a successor was not designated first, thereby relegating all other sons to branch/subsidiary status. Since a successor was not named, Grandfather remained the household head. His household remained the *honke*. Since a successor was not picked, a generational change, whereby excess sons are weeded out, could not occur. All sons were still members of the *honke*. Thus, although Grandfather established subsidiaries for his sons, these economic entities could not really be considered familial ones as well. In other words, the subsidiaries were really only subsidiaries and not branch families. Although the subsidiaries were considered a permanent aspect of the *ie*, as the enterprise, the branch families were considered only temporary entities in the *ie*, as the family. The temporary branch families could become permanent only if a successor to the headship of the main family were named. Here, we find the slippage between the overlapping planes of the enterprise and the family, creating an immense area of ambiguity and uncertainty. These two planes, the economic and the familial, were slipping apart. This increase in ambiguity and uncertainty opened the way for political processes within the organization as a whole, and as we shall see later, the processes arose from, and made use of, the various planes of reality in the *ie*.

As a sociocentric organization composed of "offices," each with its own set of duties and obligations, the *ie* is akin to the Weberian concept of a rational bureaucratic structure, wherein, as Michel Crozier wrote, "impersonal rules delimit, in great detail, all the functions of every individual within the organization. They prescribe the behavior to be followed in all possible events. Equally impersonal rules determine who shall be chosen for each job and the career patterns that can be followed."[7] Weber observed that power is also impersonalized. "Orders are given in the name of the impersonal norm, rather than in the name of personal authority; and even the giving of a command constitutes obedience toward a norm rather than an arbitrary freedom, favor, or privilege. The 'official' is the holder of the power to command; he never exercises this power in his own right; he holds it as a trustee of the impersonal and 'compulsory institution.' "[8]

In the *ie*, as in the bureaucracy, the exercise of power is legitimated in functional rather than personal terms. With authority, that is, the legitimate use of power, vested in the office rather than in the person, power and authority become subject to delimitation by calculable rules and are not open to arbitrariness, to unpredictable personal behavior. This makes for a high degree of order in organizational behavior, thereby increasing control, efficiency, and productivity. Not prone to individual irrationalities, the organization could, furthermore, exist ad infinitum. Where the institution reigns over the individual, the person simply becomes a cog in a machine, finding it impossible, as Weber aptly claimed, "to squirm out of the apparatus in which he is harnessed."[9]

We know from real-life experience, however, that whether the institution is the ideal-typical bureaucracy or the ideal-typical *ie*, the human being has a heart full of sentiments and a mind full of schemes, and even though he or she may not be able to "squirm out of the apparatus," he or she can certainly figure out how to manipulate it so that personal inclinations are acted on. Complete impersonalization is impossible.

In the Moriuchi *ie*, Grandfather acted on his personal, and highly irrational, sentiments by starting up the process of branching prematurely, that is, before designating a successor. Grandfather, therefore, bent the rules. Two important consequences arose from bending the rules. First, the high degree of calculability and predictability inherent in the sociocentric principles of the household were removed, creating a situation of immense uncertainty. This uncertainty increased Grandfather's personal control over the entire Moriuchi household, as family and enterprise. In the short run, this high degree of centralized control proved to benefit Moriuchi Industries and all its subsidiaries. Second, this increase in control came at the cost of tainting the sociocentric organization of the *ie* with the personal. Legitimate exercise of power, or authority, came to be associated with Grandfather as an individual and not with his position as household head. Authority became vested in the person rather than the office. For a while, this phenomenon did not seem to matter, but in the end, authority vested in the person proved to wreak havoc on the organizational structure of the *ie*.

Grandfather's increased personal power came from the very situation of uncertainty that he created. Premature branching meant that no son of the next generation knew whether he was to be head of the main household or relegated to branch status; premature branching, clearly not according to established rules, reduced the predictability of Grandfather's future actions, which could no longer be assumed to be delimited by his office as household head but were open to the arbitrariness of personal whim. This situation fits Crozier's conception of the relationship between power and uncertainty. "In such a context, the power of A over B depends upon A's ability to predict B's behavior and on the uncertainty of B about A's behavior. As long as the requirements of action create situations of uncertainty, the individuals who have to face them have power over those who are affected by the results of their choice."[10] Grandfather's power over his sons became total, with each son absolutely uncertain as to who would be picked as successor.

But Grandfather was stymied by his power. It, in fact, hindered his decision on succession. Because his power over his sons rendered them all absolutely obedient to him, he was never sure if they were equally competent or if one was clearly superior; they simply followed his orders. While the company that he founded became known in manufacturing and financial circles as "the peerless Moriuchi," Grandfather became increasingly unsure about its future leadership, for none of his sons had proven his merit. The proof of merit involves a certain degree of independence and risk taking, which none of them was willing to assume for fear of offending Grandfather. Regarding succession, Grandfather was certain about only one thing: Tetsuo, his eldest son, should not be allowed to assume the positions of household head of the main family and president of the main enterprise.

In 1955, the year in which Grandmother died and the first subsidiary was established, Grandfather was only one year away from official retirement as president of Moriuchi Industries. He was, however, not particularly worried about who would assume the position of president, for six years earlier he had arranged a marriage between his right-hand man, Satoo-san, and his eldest daughter, Kyoko. It was not the typical case of bringing in a *muko-yooshi*, for Satoo-san did not change his name to Moriuchi. Yet it served the same purpose. Satoo-san renounced all claims on his family of birth (which was not difficult to do since he was not the eldest son and his family of birth was not propertied). Satoo-san, already a useful member of the enterprise, was brought into the Moriuchi household as a family member, but his status within the *ie* was rather shaky, for he neither completed the full process of adoption (he did not, after all, change his name), nor did anyone assume that his position in the household was permanent.

Grandfather officially retired in 1956, naming Satoo-san as the next president of Moriuchi Industries. Grandfather would for the next nine years continue to direct operations, while Satoo-san would continue to serve as his right-hand man. Grandfather also remained head of the household, failing to decide on a successor.

Before his death at the age of seventy-four, Grandfather made it clear that Satoo-san and Kyoko were to assume the positions of household head and household wife, but only as regents. Preparing for his death, Grandfather assumed that this organizational strategy would guarantee the perpetuation of the household. The basis of such a strategy was outlined by Keith Brown: "If the head of the household dies leaving an heir who is still too young to take over the management of the household, it may be necessary to bring in someone else to help out until the heir can manage for himself. This 'regent' is frequently a younger brother of the deceased man. Once the regent's services are no longer needed he may be rewarded with a small plot of land and a house in which to establish a new branch household."[11] The sons of the Moriuchi household could hardly be considered young, for at the time of Grandfather's death, they were well into middle age. However, they were still too young in the sense of being unproven, and perhaps Grandfather felt that their proof of merit could come only after his death, when they would be released from the shackles of complete obedience. But in any case, no one had yet proven his merit to Grandfather, and so he left the crucial decision about succession to his trusted aide and son-in-law, Satoo-san.

If everything were to work according to the highly calculable, sociocentric principles of the *ie*, Satoo-san would decide which of Grandfather's sons would be most worthy of assuming the household headship of the Moriuchi *ie*, as family and enterprise. After that decision, Satoo-san and Kyoko would abdicate their positions as household head and household wife, leaving the main family to establish a new branch family in retirement (*inkyo bunke*).[12]

Satoo-san and Kyoko would be part of a new branch line, and their family would relate to the main family as subordinate to superior. In fact, Grandfather's instructions to Satoo-san followed organizational rules to a T except for one thing: under no circumstances should Tetsuo be chosen as successor.

Grandfather probably knew about the possibility of intrahousehold conflict and so he carefully planned his regency.[13] His well-laid strategy was based on others' strict observance of organizational principles. He was naive to think, however, that those principles would be observed after he had created so much uncertainty, twisted so many rules. His principal assumption was that his authority as household head could be transferred to Satoo-san as the next household head, who as regent would be allowed the legitimate exercise of power. It was an assumption that authority was vested in the office; once Grandfather left the office, the next person to assume the office would have the right to exercise power. While Grandfather was still alive, Satoo-san, as president of Moriuchi Industries, seemed to have authority, for his orders were carried out. But orders were obeyed only because everyone knew that he was acting for Grandfather; it was Grandfather's personage rather than Satoo-san's office as president that gave Satoo-san authority. Because authority had become personal and was no longer official, once Grandfather died, the relationships of authority within the household, as family and enterprise, collapsed. It was something that Grandfather had not foreseen.

The planned regency was further undermined because Kyoko, the eldest daughter, would not accept it as such. She saw the regency as her chance to assert some control over her own life. Her strategy was to have her husband fend off her brothers until one of her children acquired the necessary skills and experience to succeed. Her husband, as regent household head, would have the official authority to name one of her children as successor to the headship of the main family. Grandfather's once-obedient eldest daughter became a strong-willed and independent leader.

After Grandfather's death, Satoo-san and Kyoko were smart enough to know that their authority would be challenged by all of

Kyoko's brothers and their wives. They knew that their authority as officeholders did not come from the offices themselves but from Grandfather's personage. Now that Grandfather was dead, they were faced with a serious problem: How could they command in the absence of his personal authority? Their solution was to try to keep Grandfather alive symbolically.

On Grandfather's death, Satoo-san and Kyoko could have moved into his home, where the *butsudan* (household altar) was kept. Or they could have stayed in their home, moving the *butsudan* to their residence. As regent household head and household wife, it was their right and obligation to care for the *butsudan* and the memorial tablets contained within it. However, they did not assume that right and obligation for two reasons: (1) for fear that the other members of the household would not recognize that right and would accuse them of being mere usurpers and (2) for the need to keep Grandfather alive, so that they could continue to act in his name.

Satoo-san and Kyoko, therefore, decided to keep Grandfather's home open. It was staffed with servants, who maintained the grounds and cared for the *butsudan*. On special occasions, such as the New Year and especially *obon*, all members of the household gathered at Grandfather's home, just as they had done when he was still alive. Everyone agreed to this arrangement, for it was a convenient fiction. For the sons, it meant that a generational change had not really occurred; no one was really head of the main family, and no one was really relegated to branch status. Everyone still had the chance to assume the headship of the main family and the presidency of Moriuchi Industries. For Satoo-san and Kyoko, it meant that they might be able to maintain authority by reminding everyone of Grandfather's continued presence and of their positions as regents acting in his name.

In this situation, another plane of reality slips out: the symbolic. The *butsudan*, the symbolic center of the household, should have been placed in the home of the main family, but since no one was quite sure which of the many families was the main and which were the branches, the *butsudan* was placed in a temporary home, populated only with ghosts and servants. The *butsudan*, the symbolic plane of existence, became separated from a living household structure.

Open Revolt

Ever since Grandfather's death, Moriuchi Industries and the Moriuchi *ie* were wracked with internecine strife. The *ie*, as a concept that establishes an organizational boundary, that orders all of the experiential planes of the household, proved inadequate to hold the planes together. Two centripetal forces are necessary: authority and personal attachments. When Grandmother died, the source of warmth, attachment, and communal solidarity died. With the death of Grandfather, the vertical relationships of legitimately exercised power collapsed. The last vestiges of cohesiveness disappeared.

Since Grandfather had so much personal power over his sons, he neglected to establish organizational channels of communication and centralized control between the main enterprise and the subsidiaries. He simply saw no need. After Grandfather's death, Satoo-san's lack of personal authority and weakened official authority could not serve as the basis for centralized control. Faced with constant opposition from Grandfather's sons, he could not establish a mechanism at the main enterprise to keep track of the subsidiaries. In fact, the Moriuchi *ie* split into competing factions, each replete with its own enterprise and family: Satoo-san and Kyoko heading one, while Grandfather's sons and their wives headed their own. Yet these factions were linked by blood ties and investments.

With the breakdown in communality and the forced maintenance of relationships among the various families and enterprises, political processes developed. The basic political issue was the balance of power and dependency, a subject about which Rosabeth Kanter commented:

> Beyond the people in the most routine of functions, no one has within a small domain all of the things he or she needs to carry out

his or her job. Everyone must get things done through others who are not part of the face-to-face group in which personal agreements and informal understandings develop. There must be power tools to use in bargaining with those others who are not bound with the person in any form of communal solidarity, or else those others can keep the person in a state of dependency that renders both planning and autonomous action impossible. What makes this more bearable is that others are in the same situation, equally dependent. So long as dependencies are relatively symmetrical, people can agree to cooperate rather than trade on each other's vulnerabilities. Problems arise as asymmetry grows.[14]

Communal solidarity among the various families in the Moriuchi *ie* no longer existed. Yet as enterprises, each group depended on the others for necessary resources, for Grandfather had established subsidiaries so that forward and backward integration within one sector of the economy could occur. In other words, Moriuchi Industrial Design and Construction needed parts from Moriuchi Industries, and to make those parts, Moriuchi Industries needed devices from Moriuchi Science and Technology, and so on.

The reality of asymmetry, however, created severe problems with these relationships of dependency. Satoo-san, as regent household head and president of the main enterprise, had a disproportionate amount of power, and it was considered disproportionate only because others in the household felt Satoo-san's use of that power was illegitimate. Nevertheless, he had the official mandate (albeit in a weakened office) to decide on who would succeed to the headship of the household. In her work on corporate structure, Kanter pointed out, "People who can influence promotion and placement decisions have a source of power to the extent that people feel dependent because of the uncertainties in their careers."[15] The Moriuchi brothers were dependent on Satoo-san's evaluation of their performance, which they found intolerable.

Asymmetry also stemmed from the fact that the main enterprise, under the leadership of Satoo-san, provided the initial capitalization for the subsidiaries. Thus, Moriuchi Industries owned half of the common stock in Moriuchi Industrial Design and Construction and in Moriuchi Science and Technology. It also owned all of the common stock in Moriuchi Properties. The subsidiaries were, there-fore, dependent on the main enterprise's tacit approval of their actions, which caused further resentment among the Moriuchi brothers.

The brothers weren't merely full of bad sentiments. They were also in positions to do something with their anger. As presidents of enterprises, they held highly discretionary posts and could easily influence the allocations of resources. In his study on organizations, James D. Thompson noted that

> in all but the simplest organizations, the exercise of discretion in such a position may also enhance or threaten the action spheres of others in nearby positions. When an organization attains any sig-nificant degree of complexity, it also contains a considerable amount of interdependence among its highly discretionary jobs; i.e., deci-sions in each can have consequences for the action spheres of others in the group, and can in turn be affected by decisions taken elsewhere in the group. It is here that we would expect to find developed political processes in operation.[16]

One of Thompson's propositions about these political processes is especially relevant in the Moriuchi household: "Individuals in highly discretionary jobs seek to maintain power equal to or greater than their dependence on others in the organization."[17]

The oldest, the second, and the fourth sons used their abilities to control human and material resources in their attempt to remove the asymmetry of power in the Moriuchi household, to reduce their dependence on Satoo-san. The third son (Makoto's father) and the last simply opted out of the political processes, acting to undermine Satoo-san's leadership only through passive nonsupport.

Tetsuo, the eldest, moved to cut into Satoo-san's regency—and to cut deep. When Tetsuo's subsidiary was established, Grand-father approved a plan for initial capitalization which included the sale of a 50 percent interest in Moriuchi Industrial Design and Construction to New Nippon Appliances. As a diversified opera-tion, New Nippon's products ranged from small household ap-pliances to machinery that were of the same line as those produced by Moriuchi Industries. In this investment, New Nippon sought to gain some knowledge of Moriuchi Industries' advanced tech-nology, and Grandfather saw it as an opportunity to spread the risk of entering into a new area of business. Grandfather did not foresee, however, a turn of events, about which another of Thompson's propositions is relevant: "When the power of an individual in a highly discretionary job is less than his dependence, he will seek a coalition."[18]

Three years after Grandfather's death, Satoo-san's already weakened regency was completely undermined. New Nippon announced that it was converting its commercial base from consumer goods to heavy machinery, and in that conversion, Moriuchi Industrial Design and Construction agreed to reduce its purchases from Moriuchi Industries by over half, replacing them with purchases from New Nippon.

Rather than discrediting Tetsuo as a disloyal member of the Moriuchi household, all the other brothers used this opportunity to decry Satoo-san as an ineffective leader. After Moriuchi Design and Construction's bold move was made, Masao, the second son and the only son to have remained in the main enterprise as an executive as well as a member of the board of directors, stepped into the position of president of Moriuchi Industries, supported by his own coterie of executives. Satoo-san kept his position of *kai-choo* (chairman of the board of directors) and his position of regent household head. It was a particularly odd and embarrassing situation with all of the middle-aged men of the Moriuchi *ie* still unsure as to who would be head of the household.

Masao was an extremely astute student of household politics. Rather than try to establish control over his brothers' enterprises, he focused his energies on Moriuchi Industries and officially followed a laissez-faire policy with regard to the subsidiaries in the Moriuchi group. After a few years under his leadership, Moriuchi Industries reached record levels of sales and profits. Moriuchi Industrial Design and Construction, the renegade subsidiary, grew to capture 25 percent of its market.

During this period of prosperity, Masao completely washed his hands of any responsibility for his brothers' and their enterprises' actions, deferring from any attempt to control and offering neither personal nor financial support. Eventually, Moriuchi Properties, headed by Haruo, the fourth son, went bankrupt because it could not meet its obligations in negotiable paper that it had tendered. Since Moriuchi Properties was a wholly owned subsidiary of Moriuchi Industries, there was an unspoken expectation that Moriuchi Industries would underwrite the sale of the negotiable paper. However, there were no written agreements to that effect, and in his explanation of why Moriuchi Industries would not extend financial support to its foundering subsidiary, Masao simply reminded his executives of the group's adherence to *hoonin shugi* (laissez-faire) policies.

The collapse of Moriuchi Properties came on top of Tetsuo's resignation a year earlier as president of Moriuchi Industrial Design and Construction for the alleged misappropriation of corporate funds for personal use. At first glance, it might seem that Tetsuo had risked his position out of a taste for luxury and personal pleasure. Yet it was not merely the personal that drove him into such financially untenable positions, for it must be remembered that each brother held claim to the position of household head of the Moriuchi *ie*. Indeed, each believed that he held the household mandate, and each needed to have that mandate publicly recognized. Lavish homes, collections of European and Japanese art, and a highly visible social life were part and parcel of seeking that public recognition of status.

Through his clever use of laissez-faire policies, Masao had managed to eliminate financial competition from his brothers Tetsuo and Haruo for the position of household head. His brother Tasaburo had died, and his half-brother never presented much of a threat in the first place. Now that his brothers were in financially weak positions, Masao moved in to bring the subsidiaries, especially Moriuchi Science and Technology and Moriuchi Industrial Design and Construction, back into line. The problem, however, was that both subsidiaries were run by men who were fiercely loyal to Masao's brothers and who had participated in the history of corporate conflict.

At a celebratory dinner sponsored by Moriuchi Industrial Design and Construction, President Fujimoto, Tetsuo's former right-hand man, announced, "I would like to take this opportunity to say that if this corporation is to operate like other corporations, 50 percent of the stocks must be placed in the hands of our own corporate members and related enterprises. We have devised a purchase plan, and we will take it to the appropriate financial institutions." New Nippon Appliances had privately informed Tetsuo and President Fujimoto of its plan to divest its 50-percent interest in Moriuchi Industrial Design and Construction. President Fujimoto, in consultation with Tetsuo, saw in this divestiture a chance for independence. Masao, on the other hand, used this situation to try to break years of opposition on the part of the subsidiaries toward the parent company.

Masao, at first, resisted any temptation to exert control over the subsidiaries. Although he might have tried, given his right as the president of the main enterprise, his brothers would have countered by claiming that since he was not the household head, he had no authority to judge their actions. Although he was president of the main enterprise, each brother still had the potential of becoming the household head. Thus, the plane of the familial could be used against the economic, and for Masao, whose initial concern was to establish his authority as a leader of the main enterprise, an accusation by his brothers that he was a mere usurper would have been severely detrimental. In short, an attempt by Masao to control his brothers on the plane of the economic would have triggered a reaction on the plane of the familial, and such a reaction, in turn, would have weakened Masao's economic position.

Now that none of his full brothers was among the presidents of the wayward subsidiaries, now that they had no official position of leadership in the realm of the economic, Masao felt secure in taking strong action to consolidate the resources and activities of the enterprises within the Moriuchi group. In fact, he was forced to prove his strength as a leader by President Fujimoto's move towards greater independence. Masao had no other choice: it was now or never. He suddenly dropped his official laissez-faire policy, demanding obedience from the new, nonfamilial heads of the subsidiaries. It was a power play that he hoped would bolster his position of authority as president of the parent company.

Referring to the move toward independence by Moriuchi Industrial Design and Construction, Masao said to his board of directors, "The world sees Moriuchi Industries and Moriuchi Industrial Design and Construction as one body, and the present situation is, therefore, embarassing. Up until this time, we have owned 50 percent of the shares in Moriuchi Industrial Design and Construction, and we've had absolutely no say in its management. In this situation, Moriuchi Industries has no choice but to exert full control over Moriuchi Industrial Design and Construction by acquiring 100 percent of its shares." The world of enterprise families got wind of what was going on and delighted in this *oru oa nashingu*, "all or nothing," fight between a parent company and one of its major subsidiaries.

Before the battle could begin, however, an investigation by the National Tax Bureau revealed that monies had passed from Moriuchi Industrial Design and Construction to one of its wholly owned subsidiaries, All Japan Industrial Research Institute, which was, at that time, focusing its research efforts on toxic-waste regulations. In fact, new legislation was threatening to cut deeply into Moriuchi Industrial Design and Construction's profits, forcing the firm into a strategy of lobbying at the level of the prefectural governments. All Japan Industrial Research Institute headed the lobbying effort, using the special funds as "gifts of appreciation."

An unnamed president in the chemical industry was quoted as saying, "We're all caught in this quicksand." This statement, however, was small comfort to those who had sunk in the quicksand, to those involved in the mass resignations, including President Fujimoto and a provincial official implicated in the investigations.

The scandal brought the independence movement at Moriuchi Industrial Design and Construction to its knees. International Bank, the major creditor of Moriuchi Industries, purchased 42 percent of All Nippon Appliances' share in Moriuchi Industrial Design and Construction, and the remaining 8 percent went to financial institutions related to International Bank. Thus, Moriuchi Industries gained, effectively, complete control of Moriuchi Industrial Design and Construction. With the reorganization of stock ownership came the reorganization of reporting and control systems; at the parent company, a *kanrenkigyooshitsu* (office for associated enterprises) was created. The office was to be headed by a *boku senmu* (managing director), and its responsibilities were to include the standardization of accounting procedures, the evaluation of operational procedures and production plans, and the coordination of transfers of executives from the parent company to posts within the subsidiaries. The managing director of the newly established office stated bluntly, "The interests of the parent company are the interests of the subsidiaries."

Ever skeptical, enterprise families gossiped openly about the ability of Moriuchi Industries to centralize control. The plan was based on an almost mechanistic restructuring of the Moriuchi group. What of the human element? They predicted increased agitation at the implementation of the new controls, for the *haenuki shain* (native born or home-grown employees), those who had only known employment in the subsidiaries, would resist. After years of conflict, these executives could only see themselves as belonging to entities absolutely separate from Moriuchi Industries. Those in the know said that familial cleavages, revolving around the issue of authority within the Moriuchi household, made the establishment of a single line of centralized authority within the enterprise virtually impossible.

Masao pointedly ignored the rumors. Indeed, he displayed his confidence by moving his family into Grandfather's once-empty home. No longer was he the head of the Moriuchi *ie* in merely economic terms, for he was assuming his rightful position in the realms of the familial and the symbolic as well. Although gossips predicted continued strife, members of the Moriuchi household, even Uncle Masao's detractors, looked forward to a period of peace and prosperity.

A Mad Ringing of Telephones

Moving into the main house is not an issue that should be taken lightly, Mitsuko Itoo Nishimura told me. Her household, the Itoos, experienced some trauma after Grandfather Itoo died, for her parents had not been able to make up their minds about whether or not to move into the main house. Her mother com-

111

plained that the house was much too large and drafty and that after Grandmother Itoo died, no one adequately supervised the staff in maintaining the place. Mitsuko's mother thought that she and her husband should consider selling it. Mitsuko's father, however, was attached to the old home. Until Mitsuko's parents made up their minds, they decided to close the main house temporarily, entering it periodically only to take care of the *butsudan* or to discuss renovations with architects.

Because of one thing or another—important business in Los Angeles or a family event—the decision to move was put off for over a year. Everyone was much too busy to pay mind to the issue— everyone except Aunt Otoyo.

Mitsuko recalled events of the slow season of February one year (*nippachi*, when social and business activities come to a virtual halt in Tokyo). The Itoos were enjoying the quiet after a hectic New Year season. The dull silence, however, was broken by a mad ringing of telephones, as Aunt Emiko, the wife of Mitsuko's father's youngest brother, called Mitsuko's mother. Mitsuko's mother, in a highly agitated state, then called all of her children.

Mitsuko asked me, "Do you know what my Aunt Otoyo did? You remember my Aunt Otoyo? Sanae's mother. The one we don't like."

"Well, yes."

"Well," Mitsuko continued, "she simply walked into Grandfather's house and collected all of the ancestral tablets. My mom and my aunts were terribly upset."

"Why?"

"'Why?' What do you mean, 'Why?' Don't you see that she stole them."

I was confused and asked, "Stole what?"

"She stole the *ihai. Kazoku no kokoro da mon!*" (They're the heart and soul of the family!)

Mitsuko sounded frustrated at my complete lack of appreciation for the gravity of the event.

Apparently, on the morning of the phone calls, Aunt Otoyo let herself into Grandfather's house, simply gathered up the *ihai*, and took them to her home, where they finally came to rest in a *butsudan* she had prepared for them. Then she called Mitsuko's mother and told her, in a matter-of-fact tone, about what she had done. Aunt Otoyo said that after the New Year's celebration, which was held as always at Mitsuko's parents' place, she had a thought about the ancestral tablets collecting dust in Grandfather's unoccupied house. She felt it was rather improper to ignore the day-to-day care of the ancestors. She realized, of course, that it was no one's fault, for all of the wives, especially Mitsuko's mother, were terribly busy, given their hectic social and business schedules. Furthermore, Aunt Otoyo felt bad about being remiss herself, for she should have taken the initiative earlier to care for the ancestors. As the wife of the eldest son of the household, she shouldn't have been so selfish with her time. It was now appropriate to correct the situation, and so she would assume the daily care of the ancestors. She would assume that responsibility, as the wife of the *choonan*.

Mitsuko's mother was outraged at Aunt Otoyo's audacity, so outraged, in fact, that she called her sister-in-law to say that Aunt Otoyo had stolen the *ihai*. If, however, Aunt Otoyo had merely stolen them, it would have been easy for the wives of the household to close in on her, once again, and force her to return them to the *butsudan* in Grandfather's house. It would have been a simple, albeit tawdry, grabbing match. Instead, the other women of the household were hamstrung by Aunt Otoyo's move, for she was behaving according to the rules of, and out of an obligation to the principles of, filial piety. Instead of stealing the *ihai*, she was merely assuming the responsibility for their care. Angry though everyone might have been, the consensus was that it was a masterly move on Aunt Otoyo's part.

It must have been a smug moment of triumph for Aunt Otoyo. Ever since her marriage to Ichiroo, the eldest son from Grandfather Itoo's first marriage, her life had been made miserable by the other wives of the household. After calling her Otoyo-san as if she were a servant of the household, criticizing her taste as *hade* (garish), and denying her a proper place in the most important ritual events,

113

now, because she was assuming the care of the household ancestors, all were forced to telephone and thank her for her generosity of time and spirit.

By moving the *ihai* to her home, Aunt Otoyo and Uncle Ichiroo became the symbolic center of the household. They became established, at least on the plane of the symbolic, as the *honke*, relegating all others to *bunke*.* The Itoo household was in turmoil. The implications of Aunt Otoyo's act were indeed serious. Would it force realignment of the household? Would all of the families recognize Aunt Otoyo's and Uncle Ichiroo's claim to *honke* status? Or would they just ignore the claim and the *ihai*, cutting themselves from their illustrious past, effectively disbanding the collective household? If they did recognize the claim, would it be proper for Ichiroo to hold the title of household head without the corresponding title of president of the main enterprise? For Mitsuko's father, the question was not one of handing the presidency of the main enterprise to his older half-brother, for that he would not do. But he worried about his own position of authority within the Itoo group. What would happen if Ichiroo were to claim publicly that his rightful position had been usurped? Perhaps Mitsuko's father would be able to appease Ichiroo by allowing Ichiroo to be household head, while he maintained his position as president of the main enterprise.

There were many things to consider, strategies to map out, options to set up. But there was still a little time, for the real test of success for Aunt Otoyo's brilliant move would come in July, when

---

* Although George E. Marcus did his research among American dynastic families, I found his discussion of the dividing of personal-cum-sacred property after the death of the "founding father" to be remarkably applicable to this case. Marcus pointed out that the distribution of this kind of property is more or less left up to the descendants after the funeral, a process he described as "orderly grabbing." This acquisition, or grabbing, is a powerful instantiation of tradition, which also defines intrahousehold status. This process, Marcus noted, is orchestrated by women. See his "Spending: The Hunts, Silver, and Dynastic Families in America," *Archives Européenes de Sociologie*, 26 (1985), 237–38.

The distribution of sacred property is also a good illustration of women's work in status production. See Hanna Papanek, "Family Status Production: The 'Work' and 'Non-Work' of Women," *Signs: Journal of Women in Culture and Society*, 4 (1979) 775–81.

the *obon* ceremonies were to take place. Would all members of the Itoo *ie* defer to Aunt Otoyo's and Uncle Ichiroo's claim to *honke* status? During *obon* the Itoo *ie* reaffirms its connectedness with Japanese history, recognizing an illustrious line of male leaders, a single, unbroken line of authority. Would they all gather at Ichiroo's, where the ancestral tablets were now kept and around which the events of *obon* must take place? It was a fateful moment that Aunt Otoyo hoped to force.

In the months that followed her deed, a few noticeable changes began to occur in matters of household finance, the most significant of which was the installation of Uncle Ichiroo into the presidency of Kantoo Investment Counsellors Limited, a *yuugen gaisha* (privately held corporation), whose undervalued stocks were owned by, and traded among, members of the Itoo household only. Kantoo Investment Counsellors had been under the control of Shimizu-san, an accountant who had been trained and nurtured by Grandfather. A professional fiduciary,[19] he stepped down to make way for family leadership, to make way for Uncle Ichiroo. Shimizu-san was retained to act as an adviser and a counselor to Ichiroo, ensuring that members of the household would continue to be provided with legal, tax, and even travel services through Kantoo Investment Counsellors; he was also there to guide the investment decisions of the corporation, including those involving shares in Itoo Metals, and the management of the household's ancestral properties as well as the portfolio for the Itoo Cultural Foundation.[20] This move was negotiated jointly by Mitsuko's father, Shimizu-san, and Uncle Ichiroo, the *choonan*.

Once Uncle Ichiroo assumed the presidency of Kantoo Investment Counsellors, the women of the household began to spread rumors that he intended to push for the development, or even the sale, of properties that were particularly treasured by Grandfather, including forested mountains and open fields in northern and southwestern Japan. This, they concluded, was a sign of his disrespect for Grandfather and the household, or even worse, a sign of the decline of the great Itoo name.[21] Ultimately, Aunt Otoyo and her "influence" were blamed for Uncle Ichiroo's rumored plans.

The anticipated trauma of *obon*, however, never came because Uncle Ichiroo died in late May. In the full-scale funeral and the sumptuous grief for the death of the Itoo *choonan*, the entire household expressed its great relief.

The funeral showed an unmistakable sense of order. There was none of the confusion that had marked Grandfather's funeral: no jockeying for status, no symbolically barbed attacks, no hurt feelings. Everyone assumed his or her proper place, using Mitsuko's father as the point that defined the center of the household, for he had become, undeniably, the household head with Ichiroo's death. The executives of Itoo Metals made arrangements for the funeral, sat at the *oyakei* (all-night wake), and generally made their presence known as men beholden to Mitsuko's father, the president of the main enterprise and head of the Itoo *ie*. During the *shasoo* (public funeral) sponsored by the main enterprise, *o-erai-san* (important men in financial and manufacturing circles) turned to Mitsuko's father and said, "Shikkari yatte kudasai" (Please carry on). In that phrase came the public recognition of his status as household head and the expectation that he would act with determination to uphold the order of things. Indeed, with the position of household head came not so much the privilege of powerful men as the responsibility of maintaining the Itoo household as an enduring and developing institution that had shaped and would shape the social and personal lives of men and women.

After the funeral, the children by Uncle Ichiroo's first wife insisted that Uncle Ichiroo's *ihai* be kept with the other household *ihai*, all of which would be moved to Mitsuko's parents' residence. Aunt Otoyo would, perhaps, be allowed a copy of her late husband's ancestral tablet. For her years of suffering, she would be left with the Itoo name and a small income, dividends derived from the few shares in Kantoo Investment Counsellors that Ichiroo had left for her. It would be enough to maintain a comfortable lifestyle in Tokyo. It would also be enough to send Sanae, her only child from her marriage to Ichiroo, to college in the United States. Sanae went on to complete both college and business school, and her mother eventually joined her in New York.

6 MARRIAGE

Early in April 1981, Atsuko, Hiroko, and I were standing in the rain outside Tsunahachi Honten in Shinjuku, waiting in a queue for tables. Atsuko and Hiroko, Nobuko Moriuchi's fashionable friends, were fascinated with the demimonde, and they found me a willing escort on their outings to Shinjuku. Nobuko said that she might join us later. Night had just fallen, but already some salaried, middle-class men (*sarari-man*), were lurching in their blue-suited drunkenness out of bars in neon-bright alleys, narrowly escaping death by taxis, which roared past unnoticed by them. A mother grabbed at her young son's collar and slapped him violently across the head, ordering him to wait until they got into the restaurant to use the bathroom. The uneasy evening scene worked its way into the polite, but edgy, conversation between Atsuko and Hiroko, who clutched nervously at their pocketbooks. I stared into the puddles.

Once inside, the bustling of waiters, the loud banter of cooks at the counter, the sound of tempura frying, the entire steamy, cramped atmosphere compelled us to become a bit more relaxed, and as we focused on the first toast of the evening, the lively scene beyond our table disappeared: "To Hiroko's marriage!"

"It's not something to be congratulated about," Hiroko muttered. "Why, just looking at his face makes me ill."

Atsuko and I exchanged a quick glance, and we must have both shared the same worried thought: this is serious.

Our momentary but concentrated silence was broken when a speeding waiter tripped and spilled an entire tray of hot sake onto Hiroko's lap. After elaborate apologies from the waiter and high-pitched laughter from Hiroko and Atsuko at the mishap, Hiroko said, "I just don't seem to have any luck at all these days, do I?"

It had taken fourteen *omiai* (arranged matches) before Hiroko could finally decide to get married. At the age of twenty-seven, she was considered to be getting on in years, and the pressure of her mother's insistence on marriage had become unbearable. As a *choojo* (eldest daughter) Hiroko felt extremely close to her parents and, of course, obligated. Her mother had made it very clear to her that at this stage in her life, *oyakookoo* (filial duty) meant marriage. Furthermore, Hiroko's younger sister, twenty-three years of age, had been anxious to marry, and she would not be able to go through an *omiai* until Hiroko had been married off.

Unable to withstand the constant hounding by the women in her family and the remarks by men about the dangers of becoming a *hai missu* (spinster), Hiroko gave in to the last *omiai*. After the formal meeting, and after three informal dates, Hiroko decided that the young man was suitable for marriage. (A prospective bride shouldn't, I was told, go on more than three or four dates before deciding on marriage, for the situation becomes suspicious and may damage her chances for future *omiai*.) He was from a good Tokyo family that owned a booming real estate business, and, an even more important factor of suitability for Hiroko, he was the *san-nan* (third son), which meant that he would not succeed to the headship of the family enterprise. Hiroko did not want the responsibility and the headache of being the wife of a *shachoo* and the wife of the head of a main family. She wanted neither the formal obligations nor a life led under the ever-watchful eye of a powerful mother-in-law. Hiroko told us that she did not feel any *aijoo* (passion) for this *san-nan*, and at the time of the engagement, neither of them expected any possibility of *aijoo* in the future. However, she did feel that "somehow, things would work out for the best."

118

She was wrong. Things went awry from the very first day of their honeymoon trip to Los Angeles, San Francisco, Reno, and Honolulu—all in ten days. *Ano hito* (that person), as Hiroko called him, forgot to bring money along, but of course he told her it was her duty to take care of all the arrangements. Luckily she had brought along her credit cards and one thousand dollars in cash, which he promptly informed her was not nearly enough for all the souvenirs they would have to buy. From that very first day in Los Angeles, he called her *omae* ("hey, you"). That irritated her. Hiroko soon discovered that they really had nothing in common, and so the conversation was limited to his detailed profiles of this company president or that *shachoo-no-musuko-san* (son of a company president). That bored her. Finally, she discovered something that worried her. Hidden behind this constant conversation about up-and-coming men in enterprise was her new husband's ambition. He eventually revealed to her that although he was the *san-nan*, he stood a fair chance of succeeding to the household headship and presidency of his household's enterprise. To be considered a responsible adult male in Japanese society, to be considered for successorship, especially in competition with his elder brothers, this young man had to be married, and so, Hiroko determined, it was his ambition that carried him to their marriage. Suddenly, she saw before her a future that she had explicitly planned on avoiding.

How could her mother betray her in such a blatant manner? Hiroko's only request to her mother was that her partner in marriage not be a *choonan*. Her mother took her request literally, ignoring Hiroko's desire not to become the wife in a main family. Hiroko was deeply disturbed that her mother was complicit in this marriage, which was carried out for social, rather than personal, reasons. As *bushi* (samurai), Hiroko felt that her mother should have displayed more pride. She should have been able to rise above the purely social and the economic. Instead, Hiroko said in disgust, her mother agreed to her marriage with *tochinushi narikin* (landholding nouveau riche).

After the honeymoon, married life became even more oppressive. *Ano hito* would order food at a restaurant, and whatever he didn't like he would push onto her plate. " 'That person' never

119

shares anything that he likes." She got up at dawn just to make him *okayuu* (rice gruel) for breakfast, which he refused, demanding only tomato juice. "*His* mother told me that he must have *okayuu* for breakfast." Whenever *ano hito* wanted tea, he simply growled, "Oi, ocha" ("Hey, you. Tea").

Indeed, the small details of life had become almost unbearable for Hiroko, even more so than loveless sex, for she claimed to have at least been rather successful in avoiding the latter altogether. She told us that during her first sexual experience with "that person" she found the whole thing quite tolerable. It was only afterward, she said, that "for the first time in my life, did I experience such utter loneliness."

"And I don't want to experience that a second time," she stated calmly, displaying her cool, stoical, intentness. After only twenty-one days of marriage, Hiroko was determined to get a divorce.

"But, Hiroko, you just have to stick it out," Atsuko advised.

"I wonder about that," Hiroko sighed. "Ever since I was a very small child, my mother told me that patience is a woman's virtue. But when you think about it, don't you think that to persevere is evidence of one's lack of courage?"

Atsuko tried to counter that statement by suggesting a possible solution to Hiroko's dilemma. She suggested that she try to overcome the present situation by creating a life of her own, while still respecting her social obligations. Atsuko reminded her that it was relatively easy to be the bride of an *ii kazoku* (good family). All she would have to do is maintain appearances by attending formal occasions. "Just show your face."

Their mothers taught them the role of wife; Hiroko knew it well; and so she should just carry on: make his meals, take care of his laundry, entertain his friends, please his family. It wouldn't be hard. And if she arranged to sleep in a separate room, the question of sex wouldn't even arise. Furthermore, Atsuko quietly argued that since "that person" was extremely ambitious, he would not question what Hiroko did in her own life, just as long as that life did not interfere with his public life. "Just maintain surface appearances."

On hearing that suggestion, Hiroko sighed again and said, "But don't you think that that's terribly sad and lonely. The relationship between one human being and another disappears and becomes the relationship between husband and wife."

She continued, "At any rate, that's the basic difference between *ano hito* and myself." Apparently, "that person's" opinions about married life were restricted to statements to the effect that *nyoobo* (wife) should do this and *danna* (husband) should do that, while Hiroko tried to press the point of *ningen* (people) relating as people.

Atsuko attempted to turn that sore point into something positive about *ano hito*. His constant refrain about the duties of husband and wife probably meant that he would be a very good husband, providing for all her material needs, and if they should have children, he would probably be an exemplary father. Even if he didn't quite know how to be an *ii hito* (good person), he would probably be an excellent husband. Furthermore, as another *koko-rozuyoi onna* (secure and confident, literally, strong-hearted woman), Hiroko should be able to ignore the small disturbance in her life that he causes. "And you should create your own life, your own private space. Buck up!"

After all, Atsuko reminded Hiroko, she may have no other choice, for both households are "good" households. Thus, Hiroko could not think only about herself. She was compelled to think about her family of birth. "You really have to think about how you're going to preserve the dignity of your household."

"Families are frightening, awesome things, aren't they?" Hiroko mumbled. (Something I once heard Makoto say.)

It was nearly eleven o'clock. We had had our fill of beer and sake. The tempura on our plates was beginning to look unappetizingly cold, greasy. And it was clear that Nobuko had no intention of showing up. Hiroko insisted on paying for the bill, apologizing for revealing her innermost feelings to us. She had to return immediately, so that she would be able to greet her husband when he returned home from his late-night drinking bout. Hiroko laughed and reminded us that, after all, she was his wife.

As we walked Hiroko to Meiji Doori, a major thoroughfare in Shinjuku, she mentioned that she had called her mother out of sheer loneliness. Her mother's response to her complaints was cold, direct. All brides have the same problem. Eventually, Hiroko, too, will come to understand the value of having a husband. And when Hiroko has children, life will take on satisfaction and meaning.

On hearing this, Atsuko's tone of voice, usually soft, became aggressive, almost imperative. Hiroko, she advised, should not have children. Although their mothers could fulfill themselves by having children, she felt that to fill in the lack of affection between husband and wife with children would be a tragedy. Their mothers might have done it, but their generation was just too *wagamama* (selfish) to think that they could live lives like that. Atsuko then offered to let Hiroko know where she could get a supply of contraband birth-control pills. Hiroko laughed, telling Atsuko not to worry, for her husband—at the moment—wouldn't even attempt to touch her. As she entered her taxi, she turned a sad smile toward us and said, "Why is it that the very worst human being has to end up spending the night over?"

Atsuko and I, both emotionally exhausted by the conversation with Hiroko, decided to call it an evening, and as I made my way home, slightly puzzled and saddened, I realized that *ano hito* would always remain "that person." Hiroko never mentioned his name.

Perhaps prospective grooms view the process differently. In June 1981, Shigehisa Okubo, or "Shig" as his friends at Princeton called him, returned to Tokyo to celebrate his commencement. It had been a long struggle for him to get through Phillips Exeter and Princeton, and now he was beginning to feel as if his life were truly to commence.

Shig always struck me as a stereotypical example of the sons of the wealthy: his face immaculate, unlined, rather soft and unformed. In the United States, he complained about being mistreated because of racism. In Tokyo, he was embarrassed by the almost groveling service rendered him by his household's employees. Caught in the clash of cultures and class, he never seemed at ease.

His decision to return to Tokyo was a deliberate one. As the *sannan* of the Okubo household, he saw no chance of succeeding in the household enterprise, a chain of entertainment concerns. In fact, it was written in the Okubo *kahoo* (household code) that only the eldest son could succeed, which indeed he has. His older brother, an investment banker with an American firm, even suggested that Shig remain in the United States, go to the Wharton School of Business as he had done, and make a life for himself that would be independent of Tokyo and his household. That he could not do, for he wanted to be at ease spiritually, a state of being that would be impossible to achieve in the United States. Returning to Tokyo meant returning to himself. Commencement marked that return.

First and foremost on his mind was obtaining a position with a major trading company, so that he would both gain some business experience and reintegrate himself into Japanese society. It would be a kind of *shugyoo* (apprenticeship) for him, and it seemed his household's *kone* (connections) would get him into Mitsui. *Shugyoo*, he felt, was necessary because he was brought up spoiled. With too much "leeway" in his life, he felt that he lacked the discipline of the common man. "Improperly socialized," as he liked to describe himself, he realized that the first several months in the trading company would be difficult, not because of the work itself but because of the initiation into the world of Japanese men without the protection of his household or of status. But he was confident of at least survival, if not success, in his first experience with work. Then, he said, he would like to get married to a Japanese woman from a good household. In fact, he would like to start the process of *omiai* within the next year or so. *Omiai*, I thought, would be as a foreign a concept to the American-educated Shig as it was to me, but he rallied to its defense, underscoring it with an implicit criticism of American society.

Shig, who had a tendency to wax mystical, tried to explain to me that *en*, an invisible connection between one human being and another, a kind of karmic destiny, was involved in marriage. *Omiai*, involving a great number of people, gives *en* a chance to appear along the many avenues opened through extended relationships, community ties. *Omiai* suited Shig because many more people and opinions were involved in marriage, an institution that had more to do with a wider community than with just the immediate couple. The success of a marriage, therefore, depends not on the matching of appropriate individuals but appropriate households.

When asked what he would do if he were presented with a choice between an *omiai* partner and someone he had met on his own, Shig replied without hesitation that since he did not trust his own instincts he would prefer the *omiai* partner. There were, furthermore, other considerations that were much too complicated for him to manage on his own, including his desire to start his own business someday, in which case marriage would be a strategic factor in determining his future life in enterprise.

When asked if he didn't think that the whole process of *omiai* was rather cold, he simply replied, "No." Marriage, he told me, is important in one's life for a deep kind of companionship that isn't necessarily linked to passionate love of either the emotional or the sexual kind. And although this deep companionship between two people is important, there are other things in life that are, perhaps, more important—not just work, as opposed to the home, but aspects of one's life that are defined by the household, past and present. For example, the concern with maintaining the household's *meiyo* (honor), which is important in making a suitable match, may be more significant than companionship itself.

Americans, on the other hand, Shig declared, are extremely strange because they don't go through *omiai*. Two individuals meet, fall in love, and get married. This marriage then becomes the only way that an individual can become part of something larger than himself or herself, and because of that, Shig observed, Americans are highly unrealistic about marriage: they expect too much from that single relationship. Shig found it terribly sad that Americans have so little in their lives that they expect so much from marriage, sad that Americans must necessarily be disappointed. He seemed to have a point.

In making a match, two prospective households go through the stages of introduction, negotiation, and closure, which, Ezra Vogel pointed out, is a movement, orchestrated by the *nakoodo* (marriage arranger), through whose personal connections with both parties, the universalistic, that is, rational, aspects of the decision-making process are maximized. In essence, the *nakoodo* creates a neutral social-psychological space, in which each household can gradually approach the other and inspect its characteristics, desirable or not.[1]

The most obvious concern is that the marriage partner be healthy, that he or she not come from a genetically impaired line. Close inspection of family records is carried out to make sure also that the prospective partner has not been raised in a defective environment, indicated by incidences of suicide, divorce, crime, and the like. Beyond these considerations, however, are those of the household's economic position, which is easily determined through financial statements and a familiarity with the business press, and the household's social position, which, in turn, is determined by its affinal links.[2]

This matter of marriage and status was revealed to me by Mrs. Okimoto and her group of friends. I had first seen them at a meeting of a standing committee of the Keidanren, the Federation of Economic Organizations (the most influential business association in Japan). The debate about toxic waste was droning on and on. Bored, I scanned the audience in the gallery, high above and behind those of us seated on the floor of the auditorium. And there they were—impossible to miss in their couturier suits.

Mrs. Okimoto and her friends managed to present faces that were animated with interest. Meanwhile, their husbands who surrounded me drifted off into a sound snore. Apparently, the women were informing themselves about the issue of pollution control so that they could mount an educational program for the Women's National Auxiliary several weeks later.

The Women's National Auxiliary included wives of Liberal Democratic Party politicians, members of the Imperial Household, as well as wives of company presidents. Although the auxiliary was ostensibly concerned with environmental issues, Mrs. Okimoto said that it really differed very little from the group made up almost exclusively of wives of executives, the Association of Women in Business, whose major concerns were the education of daughters and *fuuzoku* (matters of lifestyle). Embarrassed by the fact that the Association of Women in Business was not like a professional wom-

en's association that one might find in the United States, Mrs.
Okimoto would not extend an invitation to me to attend one of
their meetings. "We're just housewives," she would say. Mrs.
Okimoto was pleased and proud, however, to ask me to attend a
meeting of the Women's National Auxiliary, especially since a talk
by a noted American scholar was on the agenda.

The women's meeting, like their husbands', was held at the
Keindanren Kaikan. The talk by the environmentalist, painfully
interpreted by a member of the auxiliary, was politely received and
quickly dispensed with. The real business, the business of *go-aisatsu*
(exchanging greetings) began when the program ended at 3:30 in
the afternoon and continued until we passed through the security
check in the lobby at 4:45. The women, at first, clustered around
Mrs. Okimoto, for she had made the arrangements for the afternoon's presentation. The women asked after one another's children, and Mrs. Okimoto proudly reported that her eldest daughter,
Reiko, found that her summer at an American university was helping her in her studies. The talk about children made up most of
the conversations, children who socialized with one another. (And
from their complaints, often forcibly so associated.)

Marriage was also on everyone's mind, for in the talk of children
the wives inevitably brought up the subject of who had gone as
an *oyome-san* to which household. The participation in the conversation about marriage was particularly keen, for an important marriage had taken place the day before. Obviously the social event
of the year, the wives who had attended the wedding politely
suggested to those who had not, "Please be sure to watch it on
television. It really was very interesting." With that suggestion
came an obvious snub, for clearly only the wives of the most elite
households were invited to the event. Among the wives who were
not invited was Mrs. Okimoto.

What I witnessed at the Women's National Auxiliary was the
interaction of women as representatives of their households in a
community defined primarily by membership in the Federation of
Economic Organizations, a community that also included the upper
echelons of the Liberal Democratic Party and "society," which
seemed to be defined by social proximity to the Imperial House-

hold. The light chatter—carried out in the most formal Japanese—about children, their educations, and matters of lifestyle belied an undercurrent of serious worrying, as each woman realized that she, her children, and her household were being inspected by the other women in the fluid process of judging household status. Status, affirmed by alliances created through marriage, made marriage a consistent topic of conversation. Marriage also defined one of the major realms of responsibility for these wives.

In Vogel's comparative study of marriage arrangers, which reached into the upper as well as middle class, the largest single group of *nakoodo* came from a women's club in Tokyo. He found that in cases of prolonged negotiations mothers were responsible for discussing the problems of *omiai* with the *nakoodo*. Fathers were, of course, involved, but mothers shaped the decisions that the fathers made by carefully controlling the kinds of information that fathers received.[3]

Vogel's findings are consistent with what I saw and heard in my informant households. Mrs. Okimoto said that for her "making a match is the most difficult thing—I really feel the burden of responsibility." Although she clearly did not enjoy the role of *nakoodo*, she had made a few matches, including those involving the children of her older brother. When her household was approached for an *omiai* involving Reiko, Mrs. Okimoto managed the negotiations with, of course, her husband's approval. For advice and information, she relied on her friends, women of the various clubs to which she belonged.

When I asked her why she thought women felt most responsible for their children's marriages, Mrs. Okimoto gave a straightforward answer: mothers are responsible for their children's educations; mothers know more about their children's temperaments and talents than fathers, from whom children are a bit distant; thus, mothers should have more say in the process of marriage than fathers. Furthermore, she reminded me, women have nothing to rely on but the family. Men may go out of the household to find employment in a bank or a trading company. "Isn't it true that they can work 'outside?' " she asked rhetorically. But women do not have that option if they want to maintain their present lifestyles and not become clerical workers. A woman has only her family. For her sake, and for the sake of her daughters, a mother must see to its continuance, protect its *meisei* (reputation), and since marriage affects the reputation and continuance of the family, it is only natural that she be the most concerned. And in Mrs. Okimoto's case, the family is the business. In fact, it was Mrs. Okimoto, caught in the trauma of an *omiai* gone haywire, who first introduced me to the importance of marriage, of *seiryaku kekkon* (strategic marriages), and of *keibatsu* (influence exercised through marriage alliances).

In early June 1980, I received an invitation to join the Moriuchis to celebrate Makoto's birthday. When I arrived, I noticed that the informal atmosphere that usually prevailed in their home had disappeared, replaced by rigid behavior and an abundance of servants who had been sent by Uncle Masao's wife. The food was elaborate and so was the dress: men in suits and women in luncheon dresses. It was the first time I had ever seen Makoto, the birthday boy, in a suit. Amidst the floral prints and starched white collars, Makoto looked most unselfconsciously chic: his long hair pulled back into a pony tail, his skin a bit too pale for the summer, his jacket a bit oversized, and everything, of course, in black. Nobuko looked uncomfortable and stiff, staying in the background with the servants, extremely quiet, neither eating nor drinking, appearing only to fill plates and glasses with fresh food and drink. Nobuko was being the perfect *ojoosama*, the perfect daughter. She managed, however, to make a face at me.

After some time had past and the guests had settled into conversational pleasantries, Mrs. Moriuchi pulled me aside to tell me what was really going on. The "birthday party" was just a pretext for arranging Nobuko's first "date" with her very first *omiai* partner, one of the guests at the party. Her partner turned out to be a young banker, someone that Uncle Masao's wife had found. (Nobuko, Makoto, and Akiko had all learned from their mother not to turn down the favors that Uncle Masao and his wife bestowed upon them. "Amaete agenasai," Mrs. Moriuchi would say. Literally, "Give them your dependency.")[4]

128

The banker turned out to be the eldest son of a university professor. He was one of what Nobuko and Makoto called the *eriito* (elite) of Japan, men who had graduated from a national university and landed a job in either the government bureaucracy or a firm in international finance or trade. I found it interesting that Nobuko, Makoto, and their mother used *eriito* in almost a pejorative sense. Clearly, the *eriito* were not of their standing, not of the inner circle that was defined almost exclusively through ties of marriage rather than middle-class notions of achievement. Thus, Uncle Masao's wife indicated to Mrs. Moriuchi that the young banker represented the best that Nobuko might be able to do in the marriage market. Mrs. Moriuchi agreed to this *omiai* because of her dependency on Uncle Masao and his wife. It was a formality that was to be endured. Nobuko consented, but she let her mother know that she was perfectly capable of finding her own partner in life.

The banker took a great deal of interest in me simply because I was an American. In an odd attempt to relieve his tension, he pulled his chair next to mine and began talking in a low, almost inaudible tone, half in English and half in Japanese, *champon* (a "mix" of cultural and conversational styles). He told me that I was lucky to be an American, for while he was in the United States as an exchange student, he had discovered that Americans were allowed to be much "freer" than he. "In Japan," he said, "life seems to be completely determined."

When I asked him what he meant by that, he replied, "Well, look at me, since I am of a certain age. I must get married." He revealed, in the kind of frankness that English seemed to permit him, that he was not, in fact, ready to get married, but he felt the pressure of his household and his supervisors at work. Switching back into Japanese, he said, "If you don't get married, it becomes difficult to handle money." Since I didn't understand the relationship between money and marriage, I asked for a further clarification, and he continued in rather forceful Japanese, "When you marry you lose your freedom, and that means that you have become responsible and can be trusted." Marriage was necessary if one were to become an *ichininmae no ningen* (complete human being), an adult.

After we had finished our luncheon, everyone agreed, as if it were a "spur of the moment" decision, to go off to a *matsuri* (festival). Uncle Masao begged off, claiming that he had a business meeting to attend, while the rest of us piled into several cars, forming a small convoy that headed from the elegance of Hatanodai to the earthiness of Asakusa, the traditional downtown area of Tokyo. Mrs. Moriuchi, Akiko and I were directly behind Nobuko and her date, while Makoto and his aunt brought up the rear.

As we kept a close eye on what was happening in the car ahead of us (Mrs. Moriuchi and Akiko observed that there seemed to be little evidence of conversation between Nobuko and the banker), Mrs. Moriuchi gave us her early impressions of him: he was certainly handsome, seemed cultured enough to speak English well, but his taste was questionable. It was much too predictable: blue suit, blue car, a Seiko watch. Mrs. Moriuchi suspected that he was the ideal bureaucrat. She also knew that Nobuko would have little time for such a perfectly boring person.

Mrs. Moriuchi was right. Nobuko would have nothing further to do with the banker. And it was left to Uncle Masao's wife to end the *omiai* process.

Later that month, Mrs. Okimoto asked me to come by her home for a private talk. She had an important favor to ask of me. Apparently, the first meeting between the Okimotos and the Hayashis, as well as the first date between Reiko and Tadashi, had gone much too well, for the Hayashi household informed the Okimoto household through the *nakoodo* that they were very interested in having Reiko come to them as an *oyome-san*. The Okimotos now needed a polite way out of the situation, so that neither the Hayashi household nor the *nakoodo* would be offended. This is where I stepped into the picture. Mrs. Okimoto asked me to make all the arrangements for sending Reiko off to New England for a summer session at some elite college, and so I called the Yale Summer School, filled in the appropriate forms, and arranged accommodations for Reiko at the Pierre in New York.

After it was determined that Reiko could enter summer session, Mrs. Okimoto asked the *nakoodo* to offer her apologies to the Hayashi household, for the Okimotos were sending Reiko off to America to further her education, at Yale no less. Strategically neglecting to say that Reiko would be abroad for only one summer, the Okimotos expressed their regrets, saying that they felt it highly improper for them to ask the Hayashis to wait for Reiko to complete her university education, especially since the Hayashis seemed concerned about finding a suitable match for their *choonan* as soon as possible. The Hayashis should, therefore, go ahead with other *omiai*.

Mrs. Okimoto needed to buy time to think about the options for her daughter's future, options that also influenced the development of the Okimoto household. Ever since the *omiai* with the Hayashis, Mrs. Okimoto had had to fend off other *omiai moshikomi* (requests for an *omiai*). Confused and overwhelmed, Mrs. Okimoto just wanted Reiko safely out of the country. Reiko, quietly pleased with her sudden popularity, left things to her mother, agreeing that a summer in Connecticut wouldn't be such a bad idea at all.

The marriage of the *choojo* of the *honke* could have an effect on the continuance of the household's "line of descent," as well as its network of alliances with other households. Reiko, who spoke German as well as English, who was well versed in the traditional arts, who was excelling in her studies, was clearly the most gifted child of the Okimoto household. Despite Reiko's distaste at the thought of marrying a *muko-yooshi*, Mrs. Okimoto saw it as a possibility, though a remote one.

"Whether a marriage is virilocal or uxorilocal," Nakane noted, "the household receiving the spouse is more eager for the marriage arrangement. There seems to be an unconscious feeling of reluctance on the part of the household which is giving away a bride (or bridegroom) since it is losing labour. Perhaps because of this, the proposal always comes from the party which is to take a spouse."[5] Mrs. Okimoto's resistance to sending Reiko off to the Hayashis' was due to two reasons. The first was the loss of talent. And the second was the loss of a daughter that she loved dearly. Mrs. Okimoto was also concerned with solidifying the Okimoto household's position in society. Mrs. Okimoto, who came to her husband's household from one that suffered heavily from the postwar reforms initiated by General MacArthur, had gone through a drastic change in status. Her marriage, she openly conceded, was a trade-off on the part of her natal household. She brought social status from a financially crippled household to a household that began thriving economically in the postwar period. Although she was extremely secure in her economic position at the time of Reiko's *omiai*, her status anxiety manifested itself in her almost frantic participation in elite women's clubs. Thus, even if the gifted and beautiful Reiko refused to remain in the household by bringing in a *muko-yooshi*, her marriage could be strategic in terms of increasing the status of the Okimoto household, perhaps bringing it up to the level that Mrs. Okimoto enjoyed in her youth.

Nakane remarked that "a household linked by marriage to a member of one's own household is considered a very important and most reliable household, and this affinal relationship has a significant function. It is the most appropriate household to ask for labour (and even financial help)."[6] In a national election, the Okimoto household, including its employees, were out campaigning for candidates from a particular faction of the Liberal Democratic party, for the wife of Mrs. Okimoto's husband's youngest brother (also involved in the Okimoto enterprise) asked for such assistance, in the name of her older sister, whose husband's brother was the head of that faction. The social, economic, and political significance of marriage alliances, therefore, was part of Mrs. Okimoto's day-to-day concerns. *Keibatsu* was not to be taken lightly.

Several weeks after Reiko had left for Yale, Mrs. Okimoto received a telephone call from Mrs. Hayashi, Tadashi's mother. It was the first time that the two women had spoken directly since the official *omiai*, when both parties gathered at the Okimoto household. Under the guise of a purely social call, Mrs. Hayashi mentioned that Tadashi had been sent to the United States on business and that it might be nice for Tadashi to take Reiko out to a Japanese restaurant in New York. Mrs. Hayashi thought it might be pleasant for both of them, especially for Reiko, since she would be without Japanese friends and feeling lonely at Yale. Caught by surprise, Mrs. Okimoto consented. And Reiko returned from her summer in New England in love with Tadashi.

Infuriated, Mrs. Okimoto forbade Reiko the company of Tadashi in Tokyo. She also called the *nakoodo* and asked him to convey an explicit refusal on the part of the Okimoto household to the Hayashi household's proposal. Unfortunately, according to Mrs. Okimoto, Reiko had been raised almost too well, as all could witness by the fact that she fell in love prematurely. As a *hako-iri-musume* (literally, a daughter placed in a box, an especially sheltered young woman), Reiko knew little, or nothing, about worldly matters, which meant that she would be perfectly happy in an *omiai* marriage. Not knowing very much about her own needs, whether social, economic, or emotional, Reiko would have left most of the decision making to her parents, especially her mother. *Hako-iri-musume*, Mrs. Okimoto told me, can usually find satisfaction, even happiness, in the *omiai* system: since they have not been allowed to have meaningful, romantic attachments with men, or even to date seriously, they tend to fall into the *omiai/ren'ai* pattern; that is, after the marriage has been arranged, the *hako-iri-musume* tends to fall in love with the man her family has chosen. In the *omiai/ren'ai* pattern, emotional and sexual immaturity allows the daughter the experience of *hatsukoi* (first love). Thus, the period between the *omiai* and the wedding itself is one of sheer bliss, for the *hako-iri-musume* is being courted by a man for the first time in her life. The problem in Reiko's case, however, was that she fell into that pattern—into deep love—without the formal announcement of an engagement.

Mrs. Hayashi, who had begun making direct contact with Reiko, sympathized with the *choojo*, telling her that it was sad to see a young woman—especially in this day and age—become a pawn in her household's plans for development. Mrs. Hayashi claimed to understand the situation and convinced Reiko that she should succumb to her heart's desires, not to those of her mother's and her household's. Mrs. Hayashi assured Reiko that she would do all in her power to see that Reiko would be able to follow her heart and marry Tadashi.

Reiko, reassured and in love, began to speak openly about her relationship with Tadashi, even to the point of calling him her fiancé. She began to make plans for a spring wedding, defying— for the first time in her life—her parents' orders. Because of this

133

situation, Mrs. Okimoto became increasingly anxious in gatherings that brought together households of the inner circle. It was, in fact, with great trepidation that Mrs. Okimoto participated in the meeting about toxic wastes sponsored by the Women's National Auxiliary, for by the date of that gathering of wives, six months had passed since Reiko's formal *omiai* with Tadashi. And since Reiko had continued to see Tadashi against her parents' wishes, Mrs. Okimoto was terribly afraid that the Okimoto household had become the subject of intense *gosshippu* (gossip). The household's reputation could become tarnished, and Reiko's, as well as her younger siblings', chances for future *omiai* could be ruined.[7]

But Mrs. Okimoto weathered the meeting of the women's club well, for there was not even the slightest hint of suspicion on the part of the other wives about her daughter's improper behavior. She still had time, she felt, to convince her daughter that the marriage would be highly inappropriate, that the Okimoto and the Hayashi households were much "too different" to form a union in marriage. This she tried to do by handing over to Reiko a report by a private detective agency that Mrs. Okimoto had employed to investigate the Hayashis' history, which appeared to be suspiciously short. Reiko grew even more distant from her mother. She became extremely polite. Obviously, Mrs. Okimoto's plan had backfired.

Mrs. Okimoto continued to be baffled by Mrs. Hayashi's skill at manipulating *honne* (the inner life of feelings) and *tatemae* (the surface world of social obligations).[8] By supporting Reiko's inner feelings, Mrs. Hayashi provided Reiko with an avenue to bring the personal into the public, and once those private feelings were expressed in the public world, the Okimoto household might be forced into a union with the Hayashis in order to protect the Okimoto household's reputation.

Reiko continued to rebel, insist on marriage—until she heard that Tadashi had consented to another round of *omiai*. Her heart and spirit broken by Tadashi's "infidelity," Reiko retreated into her room and her studies, acquiescing to her household's orders by agreeing to complete her university education and to go through more *omiai* after a long *kyuukei* (rest).

Mrs. Okimoto was greatly relieved and saddened by Reiko's decision not to go on pursuing the marriage, relieved because an alliance with the Hayashis had been avoided, saddened because her eldest daughter had to learn to suffer at a young age. An important aspect of adulthood, Mrs. Okimoto explained to me, is *kuroo* (suffering). Without *kuroo*, the character remains unpolished, undisciplined. Yet, she found it difficult to witness her daughter experience the end of *hatsukoi*, her first love. The naiveté of youth and the simplicity of passion, of romantic love, should be experienced, and with its necessary end, the young adult learns that the inner, private life of emotions, although real, is ephemeral. Mrs. Okimoto told me that she knew Reiko had discovered, as most adults do, that romantic love, *ren'ai*, cannot be counted on, cannot be the foundation on which to build one's life. What lasts, what supports, what becomes the basis of security is the household.

Reiko became increasingly withdrawn, refusing to participate in her university club activities. Her life revolved around her studies, and when she socialized it was mainly with the foreign community in Tokyo—just to brush up on her German and English, she informed us. But Mrs. Okimoto explained her actions by saying, "Her pride has been hurt." Once Reiko had exposed her inner life to society, publicly declaring her love and announcing her plans for marriage, she became trapped by societal expectations, which she could no longer meet. Therefore, she avoided contact with her circle of Japanese friends and acquaintances, taking refuge in the foreign community, where she was safe from social censure.

Mrs. Hayashi, however, provided Reiko with a solution to her dilemma. She called to inform Reiko that Tadashi still cared for her very much and that although Mrs. Hayashi knew her parents were very much opposed to the marriage, no one would make as good an *oyome-san* as Reiko. Reiko would be perfect. At this point, both Reiko and Mrs. Hayashi were consciously moving between *honne* and *tatemae*. Although Mrs. Hayashi knew that Reiko had been bitterly disappointed, she spoke of romantic affection, even with the knowledge that the surface world would shape Reiko's actions. Whereas Reiko was once motivated by romantic love, motivated by an inner force, she now was moved by pride and shame, the emotional consequences of the exposure of her inner life to society's judgment.

Quite calmly, almost stoically, Reiko informed her parents that under the invitation and approval of the Hayashis, she planned to register her marriage to Tadashi without a public ceremony, even without the permission of the Okimoto household. It was blackmail. Should Reiko go ahead with her plan the Okimotos would be known as a household defined by individual acts of preference rather than corporate interests, and they would not be considered stable. In essence, Reiko would put the future marriage prospects of her younger siblings, the future of her household's plans for development, in jeopardy. Given Reiko's absolute, almost desperate, determination, the Okimoto household capitulated and consented to a wedding ceremony.

After the engagement was formally announced, I lost contact with the Okimotos, partly because they were extremely busy with preparations for the lavish wedding and partly because Mrs. Okimoto was disturbed by the fact that I would not talk Reiko out of her plans to marry Tadashi. My phone calls to the Okimotos were answered by Mrs. Okimoto's personal secretary, who apologized profusely for the Okimotos' busy schedule and who always declined to arrange a definite date for an appointment. The period in which the Okimotos were incommunicado gave me time to participate in the activities of the Moriuchi household. It was at this time that I almost lost contact with the Moriuchis, as well as the Okimotos, through a bit of foolish indiscretion.

One evening, Makoto Moriuchi, Nobuko Moriuchi, and I were discussing my activities, which included tutoring Hideo Nonaka, the eldest son of the vice-president of United Electronics and the possible successor to the headship of the Nonaka household and the presidency of United Electronics. At the mention of his name, Makoto and Nobuko perked up, saying that he was a not-too-distant cousin of theirs: Uncle Masao's wife's sister's son. Then they asked me why Hideo needed to be tutored in English, for they knew that he had received an M.B.A. from an American university. I told them Hideo felt a little insecure about his ability to pass an advanced English language test in the construction company for which he worked. Nodding knowledgeably, Nobuko said she felt sorry for Hideo, since he was now in apprenticeship and must prove himself worthy of returning to United Electronics and to the Nonaka household as president and household head. Since he had spent so many years in America, this apprenticeship was, in fact, necessary for Hideo in order to reintegrate himself in Japanese society. To get the apprenticeship, Hideo's father had asked his younger brother, the president of United Electronics, to ask the younger brother's wife to put in a good word for Hideo at the construction company, which the younger brother's wife's natal household founded.

Makoto and Nobuko then turned the conversation to Hideo's father's younger brother's family, the main family of the Nonaka household, which had recently gone through a marriage. The eldest son had married the eldest daughter of the *honke* of a household that Nobuko dismissed as *nari-agari* (social-climbing nouveau riche). She admitted, however, that that particular household seemed to be doing well, for the eldest daughter had married into United Electronics and the second daughter into the main family of a school of traditional arts. However, she did hear that the *nari-agari* household was having some difficulty with arranging a marriage for the *choonan*.

"Oh, you mean the Hayashis of the pharmaceutical company," I said, indiscreetly.

Stunned, Makoto and Nobuko agreed that "Matto no kao wa anmari hirosugiru ne" (Matt's face was much too wide), that Matt knew too many people. It suddenly dawned on them that my identity as a *gaijin* did not necessarily keep me out of their Japanese social circle and that I may have had too much information about too many households.

Afterward I found the Moriuchis editing the content of the information they were passing on to me, saying, "Perhaps when we are all in the United States together, we might be able to tell you that, but right now, it would be a bit dangerous." For several months, I found myself trying to avoid situations, created deliberately or accidentally, in which I might be pressed into revealing information about other households.[9]

My error put my research in jeopardy, but it revealed to me a tightly knit universe of households, wherein networks are created through marriage alliances. Two informant households, the Okimotos and the Moriuchis, which I had previously thought completely unconnected, were, with the marriage of Reiko to Tadashi, within three household links of each other, within striking distance, socially.

Almost a full year after the marriage of Reiko to Tadashi, I received a letter from Mrs. Okimoto, who seemed to have settled into accepting the alliance she had once steadfastly opposed. In fact, she seemed delighted in her developing network of *shinseki* (relatives). She wrote to me in English, saying that she was enjoying the company of her new relatives and that she found Kenji Nonaka, the head of United Electronics, to be brilliant and witty. She was also enjoying the gala events sponsored by United Electronics, to which all relatives were invited.

The Okimotos were related to the Nonakas through Reiko's marriage to Tadashi. Makoto and Nobuko Moriuchi were related to the Nonakas through their aunt. Both the Okimotos and Moriuchis were considered relatives by the Nonakas, and as time passes, and with the centrifugal force of events, ritual and recreational, centered around the Nonaka household, the Okimotos and the Moriuchis, at opposite ends of the *shinseki* network, will likely approach each other and become firmly positioned on each other's social horizon.

The network that the Moriuchis and the Okimotos entered with the marriage of Tadashi and Reiko is at once (1) a pathway by which the households could approach each other through personal ties, (2) a boundary that defines the social-psychological space within which they make their approach, and (3) a measure by which they could gauge social distance when making an approach. This structure of boundaries and measured pathways within them is, furthermore, far from static. It pulsates with activity, as individuals are drawn from one network center to the next.[10]

The breadth of the *shinseki* network, furthermore, varies widely, depending on, as Chie Nakane noted, the ability of households to maintain constant intercommunication and to perform the duties defined by *shinseki* relationships, which include the exchange of gifts during, and perhaps attendance at, major life-cycle events, such as weddings and funerals, in any household within the *shinseki* network. All of this depends, furthermore, on the household's economic position.[11] Since the maintenance of *shinseki* relationships incurs considerable expense in ritual gift exchange alone, it is no wonder that most networks of *shinseki* extend only one link outward, only as far as households of bilateral first cousins, from any single household. The Moriuchis and the Okimotos, given their immense wealth, could enter into a network that defined *shinseki* as those households within two, and perhaps three, links outward from any single household.

The discovery of the concept of *shinseki* and the active pursuit and maintenance of *shinseki* relationships among my informant households confused me, for the sudden appearance of *shinseki*— a set of real, live affines—contradicted my understanding of household structure. People were supposed to marry out, to assume corporate positions, to cut ties with their families of birth, yet *shinseki* seemed to be at the center of the way my informants organized their social lives beyond the immediate boundaries of their particular households.

The concept of *shinseki* ignores the ideological and sociological significance of corporate membership. Instead, it presumes that although a person has assumed a new position through marriage, leaving his or her old one behind, he or she as an individual, that is, as one without corporate recognition, still "belongs" to his or her natal household.

Because *shinseki* relationships rest on individuals rather than on corporate positions, those relationships are temporary, ephemeral. Thus, Nakane wrote: "In the Japanese system, the *de facto* and *de jure* relationship with a household of affines usually rapidly decreases after the death of the individual member through whom the affinal relation is established. Close relationship with households of affines is kept through individuals, not through a kinship network as a whole."[12] Corporate positions exist beyond the life of an individual; therefore, corporate relationships are permanent, whereas those based on individual ties are not. Thus, an *ie* such as the Moriuchis, made of up positions in the *doozoku*, can exist for almost five hundred years, but its network of *shinseki*, made up of individual ties, changes with each generation. Permanence within the *ie* and flexibility in its relationships with other households allow the nature and quality of alliances among households to escape from rigidity and atrophy and to develop with changes in status that come with changes in Japanese society and the economy. This kind of flexibility, of course, allows for the continued existence of the *ie* as a corporate institution, a permanent body.

But what makes *shinseki* relationships work? Stated simply, it is difficult to cut ties of flesh and blood. No matter what the restrictions for corporate membership, no matter what the dictates of society, a parent feels strongly for his or her child. Are we, then, placing the biological and emotional back into familial patterns? If so, are we not contradicting what we know about the *ie*?

The answer to these questions lies, again, in the concept of the *ie*, which provides a single style of articulation for the various planes of life: the corporate and the individual, the institutional and the biological, the social and the emotional. As the basis for a style that expresses and shapes life's experiences, the concept of *ie* presents not an oversimplified design, but one that, in its sophistication, plays on oppositions. Every member of every household is placed in every moment of the day in experiences that are defined by *ie* and *uchi*, *giri* and *ninjoo*, pulled by the opposing themes of social demands and intimate concerns, and in that movement, social life in the household, as family and enterprise, comes to be.

In a virilocal marriage, the bride's dual allegiance arises from this thematic opposition. Jane Bachnik pointed out, for example, that the bride has moved from one *ie* to another. In terms of formal and obligatory relationships, she is socially distant from her household of birth, yet she is emotionally close to members of that household.[13] In her new *ie*, she has assumed a socially recognized, corporate position, yet she is emotionally detached from members of her new household. Pulled between corporate membership in her new *ie*, from which she derives the recognition of social standing, and emotional belonging in her old *uchi*, from which she derives the solace of familial love, the bride comes to be the crucial link between households. *Shinseki* are, in fact, a structural manifestation of this movement between *ie* and *uchi*, a linkage of households through the social and emotional ties that bind. The dissonance between societal demands and personal needs becomes acute for a bride in her new household because she, as a newly recruited permanent member, is socially close but emotionally estranged. Thus, the bride is forced, at once, to remain in her new household in recognition of corporate obligation *and* to return to her former household in acquiescence to personal inclination.

One month after her marriage to Tadashi, Reiko's "return" to her emotional home, her private *uchi*, was imminent.

7 LOVE

For some unknown reason, perhaps just to confide in someone, Mrs. Okimoto had decided to reestablish contact with me,
and over lunch in her home we discussed in detail the anguish
that Reiko's wedding caused her. She told of the pain of having
to maintain *tatemae* among the guests at the ceremony—bankers,
politicians, presidents of manufacturing concerns—while feeling
deeply an emotional resistance to the marriage. That resistance was
apparent, for Mrs. Okimoto had kept Reiko's former bedroom
open, just as Reiko had left it. The message to Reiko was clear: the
Okimotos had never approved of her marriage and had not, in fact
let her go—at least in the realm of *honne*.

Mrs. Okimoto said that ever since the marriage she had had
almost no contact with Reiko, only one telephone call from her.
On the one hand, Mrs. Okimoto found this situation to be strange,
for it felt as if she had raised someone who had "mattaku tanin ni
natta" ("become a total stranger, an outsider"). On the other hand,
Mrs. Okimoto fully expected a social distance between her and
Reiko, especially since Reiko had married a *choonan* and, thus,
would be extremely busy and under a great deal of stress, trying
to fit into the Hayashi household, to become a full-fledged member
of her new *ie*. Although a bit resentful that there was so little news
from Reiko, Mrs. Okimoto could not help but feel sorry for her;
the life of an *oyome-san*, she told me, was difficult, even miserable.

Reiko's one telephone call since her wedding was just the beginning, Mrs. Okimoto felt, of many, many more to come. Reiko said that her adjustment to life in her new household was proceeding smoothly, better than she had expected. From the politeness and distance in her manner of speaking, from the slight trembling in her voice, Mrs. Okimoto knew, however, that Reiko was straining under the pressure to be the perfect bride. And, in fact, Reiko had called to thank her mother for helping her with a perfect start to the assumption of her new position: the ritual display of her trousseau had gone very well, and Mrs. Hayashi apparently was immensely pleased with what Reiko had brought along to her new household.

The assemblage of the trousseau, of course, had been Mrs. Okimoto's responsibility. She included: a set of Western porcelain and silverware; a set of Japanese dinnerware, including lacquer; linen of all sorts, tablecloths, napkins; silk futon covers; and in the seven *tansu* (chests), new kimono, obi, and jewelry. Of what Mrs. Okimoto was most proud, however, was the inclusion—on the very top of the first drawer in the first *tansu*—of the Okimoto *mon* (household crest), a geometric design simply embroidered on a plain piece of cloth: it was meant for Reiko.

Mrs. Okimoto heard about the trousseau's positive reception by Mrs. Hayashi with great relief. Not only did the trousseau reflect Reiko's good breeding and, perhaps, Mrs. Okimoto's pride in her household, but it was the only way that she could help her daughter adjust to, and become accepted by, her new household, especially her new mother-in-law. At the time, the careful selection of items for the trousseau was all that Mrs. Okimoto could do for her daughter.

Obviously empathizing with Reiko, Mrs. Okimoto began telling me about her experience as an *oyome-san*. After her honeymoon, she returned to an apartment that had been closed. The separate residence, which she had been promised, was not forthcoming. Instead, all of her trunks had been moved to the Okimotos' main house, where she was forced to take up residence with not only her husband but her parents-in-law and her husband's younger, unmarried siblings. Because the household was a *shooka* (merchant house) and very traditional in its ways, she found herself in a residence full of people, including *sumikomi*, those who had come to work and live with the Okimotos.

Because she was the newest member of the household, she ranked only one step above the servants. Every morning etiquette required that she arise before her mother-in-law—which meant the day began at 4:30—and start preparing breakfast with the maids, a meal for sixteen or seventeen people. She remembered how humiliating her first few breakfasts were. She had to sit on her heels away from the table so that she would be able to stand quickly to retrieve the empty rice bowls and serve freshly filled ones. Although exhausted by her early morning duties, she never allowed herself a nap, for fear that others would besmirch her character, accusing her of indolence.

Life was so miserable that she thought of running away, of returning to her parents, every day. Her only escape, however, was the telephone, secret calls to her girlfriends. Yet unmarried and still at college, they advised her to get a divorce. One day she packed a small suitcase, determined to return to her "home," but she made it only as far as the train station, where she was overcome with vertigo; in the early morning darkness, the faces of Mother, Father, and her younger brother appeared before her. She felt the rush of shame for the notoriety that her "home" would acquire were she to go ahead with her "selfish" plans; the shame was even more intolerable than the distaste she had for life in her new household. Sick to her heart, she returned to the Okimoto household and the countless bowls of rice at breakfast.

Life did become easier for her with the birth of her first child and as she adjusted to the ways of her new household. It became especially easy with the death of her mother-in-law. But for many years afterward, her only source of solace was the private conversations with her mother, for whom she never lost her tremendous respect and from whom she received not only advice but empathy. A mother knows the hardship of life as an *oyome-san*, and for this reason, Mrs. Okimoto was certain of Reiko's "return." Despite the deep disappointment that Reiko caused her, Mrs. Okimoto was determined to do all she could to help her daughter through this miserable, but necessary, period of suffering.[1]

The bride, as the newly recruited member of the household, faces suspicion as an "outsider." Each household is considered so distinctive in its lifestyle and customs that a bride is expected to undergo a great deal of hardship to adjust to the *kafuu* (ways) of her new household. The pointed comments by her mother-in-law about her maladjustment often serve as a reminder that she still has to prove herself, demonstrate her willingness to give up her past ways, her former household. Nakane wrote of the rivalry between mother-in-law and daughter-in-law, which is almost fabled in Japanese culture:

> The relationship between the mistress and her successor often involves hostility. The son, being the successor of the father in this type of residence, will occupy the role of the father as the head of the household, so that the mother looks to him as a surrogate for her husband, on whom she can depend entirely. But the son's role as husband to his wife is often overlooked by the mother. In fact the son placed in such a position has to face the conflict of his roles as son and as husband. The most difficult situation arises when he has a weak personality and is therefore torn between mother and wife. This situation places these two affinal women in jealous competition centered on the man, in which the mother usually dominates the newly arrived young wife.[2]

A bride who has arrived at her new household through *omiai* knows little if anything about her husband, and given his emotional alliance with her mother-in-law, she is, in fact, shut out emotionally and forced to return, if only through telephone calls, to her household of birth to seek the solace of familial love.

In her structural position, a bride lacks not only love but power. As a newcomer—indeed, as a stranger—she is strapped by strict obedience to her mother-in-law and has no one to represent her interests other than herself. As a stranger to the household, one not yet to be trusted, she speaks with a weak voice. Her husband, from whom she is also distant, will not serve as an effective ally, for he is caught between the roles of husband and son. In fact, closer emotionally to his mother than his new wife, the husband shuts out the bride politically.[3]

The bride learns that initially the social and material resources necessary for establishing power in her new household are not available internally, but externally in her household of birth. She brings with her the power derived from *keibatsu* (influence exercised through matrimonial alliances). As Mrs. Okimoto knew well, if your husband's household, as family and enterprise, is heavily indebted to a bank of which your older brother is president, then you have power in your husband's household. When financial or social problems arise, it is with eagerness, albeit not completely unmotivated by self-interest, that the bride offers to seek the help of her natal household. Given her position as the link between two households and her powerlessness, the pursuit of aid from her natal household for her husband's household makes complete sense. Perhaps that is why households believe that *shinseki* (households of affines) are the most appropriate households to ask for aid.[4]

Once aid is given from one household of affines to another, relationships of *giri* come to be, wherein one household is obligated to another and the acceptance of one favor necessitates the return of another. This becomes a routine cycle of cooperation, but its beginning, its motive force, comes from the bride, whose structural position deprives her of love and power and provides a possible solution to her personal dilemmas.

As the bride adjusts to the ways of her new household, thereby proving her loyalty, and contributes to its economic and social welfare, she strengthens her position and eventually assumes the position of leadership that her mother-in-law once held, that is mistress of the household.[5] This process of increasing status for the bride is evident in the success of Mrs. Okimoto's household "career." Vibrant and self-possessed, she was clearly a moving force in her household. It is hard to imagine that this *kokorozuyoi onna*, this immensely confident woman, was at one point in her life dominated by a mother-in-law, that she was a young bride reduced to tears after serving endless bowls of rice at breakfast. She sits on the board of directors of Okimoto Paper Products, taking part in major decisions and earning a reputation as the most difficult board member to convince of the value of major changes in product lines.

In lifestyle, she is completely independent of her husband, seeing him only one or two evenings a week, unless, of course, formal events call for a higher frequency of joint appearances. She even maintains a separate residence, a four-bedroom pied-à-terre in central Tokyo in an apartment complex adjacent to her mother's home. It is her escape from the responsibilities of being mistress of a household. Of course, Mrs. Okimoto's rise in the Okimoto household was due to her obvious intelligence and business acumen, but the fact that she served as the affinal link between households—the strength of her *keibatsu*—in complementary sectors of the economy cannot be ignored.

Networks of households, *shinseki*, with brides as links and *keibatsu* as the operative force, are derived not from the bride's gender per se but from her structural position within and between households, between that of corporate membership and of birth. The role of *muko-yooshi*, a son adopted through marriage, an adopted husband, makes clear the importance of structural position.

The groom in an uxorilocal marriage is an in-marrying affine, and as such, we may refer to him as a male bride. Among Keith Brown's informants, the parties in marriage were described as the "sending side" and the "receiving side," rather than the groom's side or the bride's side. It made no difference in terminology whether the sending side was providing a bride or a *muko-yooshi* for the receiving side. In terms of *yuinoo* (betrothal gifts), the receiving side paid a sum of money to the sending side, whether a male or female was sent. In terms of relationships between households, reciprocal social obligations and ritual responsibilities were the same, whether the marriage that brought two households together was virilocal or uxorilocal.[6]

With respect to power and status within the household, Brown found similarities between the bride and the *muko-yooshi*:

> There is—nothing to suggest that the adopted husband is anything other than an in-marrying affine. Because he is a male and performs

male roles, he shares many features with a son. But because he is
an in-marrying affine, he also differs from a son and, accordingly,
has some similarities with an in-marrying bride. Even in the areas
of authority where men normally dominate over women, the
adopted husband differs from a son. Henpecked husbands exist even
in male-centered Japan, and it is assumed as a matter of course that
the wife will "wear the pants" much of the time in a household with
an adopted husband.[7]

Although Nobuko Moriuchi could drive me crazy with her big-
sister bossiness, I found myself spending a great deal of time with
her during the summer of Makoto's departure for Princeton. Makoto was suddenly caught up in a whirl of appearances at formal
events at both the household's main enterprise and at the subsidiary that his deceased father had headed. Nobuko felt the early
effects of deprivation of his company and simply needed to talk
things through with somebody.

On a long walk through Shibuya, Aoyama, and Roppongi, poking into boutiques and stopping at cafes to escape the heat and
humidity, Nobuko told me that Makoto's acceptance at Princeton
had turned out to be a mixed blessing for him. Although it would
give him a chance to get away from Tokyo and to experiment with
life and learning, it also brought him into the limelight. Once
thought of as "that weirdo," he was now recognized as possibly
the most promising young man of their generation. Now, with his
intelligence validated by acceptance at an Ivy, the household was
full of expectations for his future. He could no longer escape
unnoticed.

The night before my walk with Nobuko, Makoto had been invited
by Uncle Masao to dinner. Uncle Masao announced that he would
personally look after Makoto's interests, completely financing his
education in the United States. Nobuko said that Makoto was terribly upset by this offer that he could not refuse.

Makoto's mother and the present president of Moriuchi Science
and Technology, his father's former right-hand man, were ecstatic
over Makoto's academic success—and over the possibility that
Makoto might be groomed for taking over the household, as family
and enterprise. His mother had repeatedly suggested that if Makoto
were willing, it would be good for him, for he would assume a

position of leadership, wealth, and power. It would be good for
his mother, for it would not only vindicate her husband's unsuc-
cessful attempts to succeed, but also raise her status within the
household and in society at large. It would be good for his two
sisters, especially Nobuko, for Makoto would be able to look after
all her needs, no matter whom Nobuko might happen to marry.
And finally, it would be good for the families of those men who
were deeply loyal to his father while he was president of Moriuchi
Science and Technology. It was good for everyone except, it
seemed, Makoto. Makoto had no intention of staying in the family
business. He wanted to write. And after Princeton, he planned on
moving to New York. Tokyo was not for him.

"My poor mother," Nobuko said. "She raised such crazy kids."

"What about you, Nobuko? Would you ever consider staying
with your mom and marrying somebody who could join the
business?"

"Are you kidding? A *yooshi*? You saw how terribly I did with
that banker. I can't even go through an *omiai*. How can anybody
think that I could do that. Anyway, everyone has given up on me.
I'm free to do as I please."

Nobuko didn't think that anyone expected her to be clever
enough to manage a *muko-yooshi*. If the daughter isn't clever
enough, Nobuko continued, the *muko-yooshi* might *hairi-sugiru* (enter too deeply) into household affairs. The daughter that brings in
a *muko-yooshi*, therefore, must not only manage his career, that is,
make him acceptable to the wider community as well as his new
household, but she must also protect her household from his potentially disruptive behavior.

A *muko-yooshi*, like most men, Nobuko pointed out, is driven by
his desire to achieve at least a modicum of financial success. The
difference between a *muko-yooshi* and other men, however, is that
he is willing to find success through marriage, through a kind of
marriage that would mean giving up his household's name, giving
up his position within his household, and assuming a position in
his wife's household, thereby cutting off ties with not only the
living members of his household of birth but his household's his-

tory, with his ancestors, as well. What kind of man would do that? A man, according to Nobuko, who is driven by personal ambition. A *muko-yooshi* might be so ambitious that he would be driven to the point of placing his individual interests before those of the household's as a whole. Admittedly, *muko-yooshi* are necessary for the continued existence of households, but unfortunately, as *tanin* (outsiders), they can never be fully trusted. Thus, a woman who agrees to bring in a *muko-yooshi* assumes an immense burden. In many respects, she is sacrificing her personal life for the sake of her household. According to Nobuko, her situation epitomizes the situation of women in family enterprise, at once immensely powerful and terribly weak. By denying her own personal inclinations and succumbing to the household's needs, she assumes, in fact, a position of power.

Like an *oyome-san*, the *muko-yooshi* faces emotional estrangement as an outsider, a *tanin*, in the household in which he has assumed corporate membership. His position, however, is worse, for he faces not only the problem of trust but also the problem of respectability. When I asked Nobuko if she knew of any cases in which a *muko-yooshi* had overcome this dual problem of trust and respectability, she told me about the Muramoto household, which had just brought in an "outsider" to head it, denying the *choonan* successorship in the Muramoto *ie*.

The Muramoto case did not follow exactly the standard form of marriage and adoption, for although the eldest daughter's husband was chosen as successor to the household headship and next president of Muramoto Concern, he did not assume the Muramoto name. Instead, the eldest daughter of the Muramoto household took her husband's name. In every other respect, however, the marriage resembled that of a *muko-yooshi*'s: the *josei* (daughter's husband) moved into the position of successor in his wife's household; she, not he, would be expected to assume the responsibility for Muramoto household properties, including the largest bloc of common stock owned by an individual in Muramoto Concern; her children would not be considered *soto mago* (outside grandchildren), children outside the household "line," but grandchildren of the Muramoto *ie*, who would be expected to assume the Muramoto name; and, finally, these grandchildren of the Muramoto household would be considered for successorship in the next generation.

When the engagement between the *choojo* of the Muramoto household and Katoo-san, the second son of the Katoo household, was announced, it made the major dailies, which ran charts outlining the network of *shinseki* that the Muramoto household would be joining through this marriage. The charts included Katoo-san's natal household, whose head was a high-level government official, but focused primarily on Katoo-san's mother's natal household. The display of *shinseki* in the charts (which, by the way, is standard practice when an important marriage is announced) began with the Muramoto household, proceeded on to the Katoo household, and on to Katoo-san's mother's siblings' households of affines and *their* households of affines, sketching, therefore, a *shinseki* network with a breadth of five household links. From the charts, the public learned that of Katoo-san's mother's siblings, the brothers were chief executive officers of manufacturing concerns, while the sisters had married politicians and high-level bureaucrats. Through one of the sister's marriages, the Katoos were related to the chairman of the board of a major bank. My informants pointed to that marriage as one of the finest examples of *seiryaku kekkon*, strategic marriages.

Unlike the Moriuchi household, which had developed its enterprise along the lines of vertical integration, the Muramoto household divided Japan into northern, central, and southern territories, the central region controlled by the main enterprise and the northern and southern by two separate subsidiaries. Each enterprise placed most of its efforts into the manufacture and marketing of a single product line. A few years before the announcement of the engagement between the Muramoto's *choojo* and Katoo-san, Muramoto Concern's success at this strategy of horizontal integration brought its operations under investigation by the Fair Trade Commission. The commission, furthermore, was within Katoo-san's father's sphere of influence.

Attesting to the ineffectiveness of the Fair Trade Commission, the marriage between Katoo-san and the Muramoto's *choojo* had nothing to do with the commission's investigation. The Muramoto household was capable of solving the legal problems on its own.

The marriage between Katoo-san and the Muramoto *choojo* was strategic for reasons internal to the Muramoto and Katoo households. In the Katoo household, there were two sons and two daughters. The eldest son had already been chosen as the successor to the household headship and was being groomed to follow in his father's footsteps, which meant that the *jinan*, the second son, had to be properly "placed." Katoo-san, the *jinan*, had been trained as a scientist and employed by Muramoto Concern's main enterprise for many years before the announcement of his engagement to the president's eldest daughter. In that time, he had proven himself to be extremely capable. In the arrangement of the marriage, the Muramoto household solved the problem of leadership in the next generation, and the Katoo household placed their second son into a position that would curtail any envy he might have of his elder brother's position, for the *jinan* would be entitled to become the president of a major manufacturing concern. Although the *jinan*'s children would "go over" to the Muramoto "line," he would still maintain dignity because he would be allowed to keep his natal household's name.

Soon after his marriage to the Muramoto *choojo*, Katoo-san, even as a newly recruited member, began to prove himself worthy of the Muramoto household's trust and respect. He began by playing an important part in solving another internal problem: what to do with the Muramoto *choonan*, who had been ousted, effectively, by his elder sister and by Katoo-san. Katoo-san requested that his father use his personal ties to make arrangements for the *choonan* to study at Cornell as a special student. Although he would receive no degree, on his return he could begin employment "outside" the Muramoto household with pride, claiming to have studied at a leading American school of engineering.

When I met the Muramoto *choonan*, he did, indeed, take a great deal of pride in having attended Cornell. He spoke with enthusiasm about his job with an engineering firm and his exploits on overseas projects. When I asked him if he were interested in returning to his household's enterprise, he replied in the negative, saying that

153

he would like to "make it on his own," that he wanted to prove himself as a "professional." He displayed the effects of a very neat process of resocialization: from *choonan* to professional. Later the Moriuchis told me that because of pride he would never ask to return to Muramoto Concern and, from what they understood, he could return only if his older sister, Katoo-san's wife, were to ask for his help in directing the enterprise. When I asked if they thought she would, they agreed that she would not, for as the Moriuchis well knew from their experience with a long successor struggle, an eldest son who is not chosen as successor but is allowed to remain within the household could be potentially disruptive, using his position within the family for his own purposes and undermining lines of authority within the enterprise. The Muramoto *choojo*, they agreed, would hold on to her position of power and authority within the family and the enterprise.

Katoo-san proved himself worthy by solving not only problems internal to the Muramoto household as family but also problems of the household as enterprise. What the Fair Trade Commission's investigation showed Muramoto Concern was not the danger of having too large a market share, for the commission proved to be ineffective, but that Muramoto Concern had reached a point of market saturation. With Katoo-san able to ask their recently extended, and influential, set of *shinseki* for advice and aid, the Muramoto household decided to enter the Latin American market. The Muramoto *choojo* and Katoo-san moved to São Paulo, where he became the first president of the South American division of Muramoto Concern, earning the complete respect of the Muramoto household.

"What about the marriage itself? Did the Muramoto *choojo* agree to it willingly?"

"Oh, no," Nobuko Moriuchi told me. "But she must be happy now."

The position of a newly recruited member entails a paucity of resources, which compels the member, whether *oyome-san* or *muko-yooshi*, to return to her or his natal household. By drawing on the external, the *oyome-san* and the *muko-yooshi* eventually gain a position of strength within their new household of corporate membership. In many ways, the *oyome-san* and the *muko-yooshi*—both caught in structural positions of weakness—are similar. There is, however, one important difference: the woman has available to her an important, internally derived source of power not available to the man, and that is the ability to bear children.

Although the principles of patrilineal descent are routinely ignored in the process of succession, a woman who bears the next heir and successor advances in her household career. Prestige comes from giving birth to the next head of the household and president of the enterprise. The child also becomes available for an alliance within her husband's household, thereby changing the household's internal balance of power.

Birth

Mitsuko Nishimura (née Itoo) showed me the power of maternity, as I observed her decide to have a child and go through the processes of pregnancy, birth, and child rearing. Mitsuko and I had been friends long before I learned to speak Japanese. We met while we were in our early teens, standing on tables in the cafeteria of Sacramento State College, singing "We Shall Overcome." Our older sisters were best friends and roommates, and they seemed to enjoy organizing demonstrations.

Mitsuko and I thought Sacramento the greatest city in the world, and we admired our sisters: independent, opinionated, and smart. (Later in life, as Mitsuko and I recalled those days, we would both imitate our sisters in the particular way that they adjusted their matching hornrimmed glasses and said: "Oh, how bourgeois. . . . ") Much to Mitsuko's parents' chagrin, Mitsuko took after her older sister.

Immediately after her graduation from Tsuda College, the "Bryn Mawr of Japan," Mitsuko was put through several *omiai* by her parents, which she sabotaged by being much too forceful and confident in her presentation of self. She simply scared away the prospective grooms. She wanted a career, any career. And so she set off for San Francisco on an adventure and found not a career but love.

In California, Mitsuko met George, an American graduate student, with whom she spent several romantic summer weeks, traveling across the country on a motorcycle. George was on his way home to the Carolinas, and Mitsuko thought she would join her older sister, who had established herself as a graphics designer and printmaker in Bucks County, Pennsylvania. Late in the fall, Mitsuko suddenly appeared on the stoop of my apartment building on College Avenue in Ithaca, where I was an undergraduate at Cornell. She said that she needed to talk to me and to rest up a bit before she left for home. Things had not worked out as she had expected. She had been lonely in Pennsylvania, and her sister had been too busy with a new project to pay her much attention. Then she had gone off to find George—a wrong move.

In the Carolinas, George had told her, "Don't say you love me. Love is meaningless. People even say they 'love' their pets." The romance was over, and Mitsuko felt compelled to return to Tokyo, where she was hospitalized for hysteria and a severe loss of weight. A year later, her entire family and a guest, a young executive in the household enterprise, visited my family in Hawaii. Under the pretext of a vacation, Mr. and Mrs. Itoo were trying to convince Mitsuko to marry their guest, Mr. Nishimura. The *omiai* in Tokyo had gone well, and their first chaperoned date was the trip to Hawaii. Soon after their return to Tokyo, Mitsuko married Mr. Nishimura.

When I saw her again in 1979, the once-raucous Mitsuko had turned into a demure, proper wife, living in a spacious home in the elegant neighborhood of Koojimachi. She had given up her plans for a professional career, deciding instead to live the life of a housewife. She amused herself by instructing the neighborhood children in the violin, English, and French. But, she said, "It took some time before I gave up." She knew that her older sister, Izumi Westgate, was disappointed in her, but what she experienced in the United States frightened her. Furthermore, she didn't think that Izumi's life was all that great: Izumi married a photographer, who then left her; Izumi's life as a single woman and as an artist seemed intriguing but lonely to Mitsuko.

"You're studying family enterprise? How strange," she said. But because my research touched on her life, she soon took great interest in the project and enjoyed telling me about her experiences with Itoo Metals, her household's enterprise.

Mitsuko considered Itoo Metals *her* household's enterprise because of the circumstances of her marriage. Although she had taken her husband's name, most of the property in the marriage, including their home, was held by her, for the Itoo household had provided for the marriage completely. Mitsuko had not yet left her natal household. When Mitsuko was introduced, for example, she preferred to be called Itoo-san, rather than Nishimura-san. On her mailbox, the name Itoo came before Nishimura. Clearly the question of successorship had not been decided, and all the children in the Itoo household were still eligible, all except Izumi, of course. Mitsuko admitted that there was some tension between the Itoo siblings, but she refused to participate much in the rivalry, for she believed that the decision was really her parents'. Neither she nor her two brothers could do anything about it. Mitsuko merely wanted to be left alone, to tend to her home, her husband, and her pregnancy.

On the birth of a child, a girl, her parents, not her husband's, showered Mitsuko with gifts, but nothing seemed to compensate for those first difficult weeks after her return from the hospital. They were traumatic. Whenever the maid left for the evening and Mitsuko was left alone with the baby, she was stricken with terror, for if the baby coughed or refused to eat, Mitsuko would become absolutely certain that it was going to die. The baby seemed so small, so weak. All of Mitsuko's energy was channeled into restraining a feeling of panic. She had to keep herself from running off to the hospital every time the baby cried. Mitsuko hated all the trouble and worry that the little girl caused.

A full year later, just before the Girls' Day Festival, I spent one of many quiet days with Mitsuko and the baby. It was extraordinarily restful. The panicked resentment that Mitsuko felt toward

Keiko-chan, the baby, had given way to tender coddling. In the kitchen of her Koojimachi home, while we were preparing lunch for ourselves, Mitsuko admitted that she was once disappointed with Keiko-chan. When Keiko-chan was first brought to be breast-fed, Mitsuko couldn't believe how ugly she was, red, wrinkled, small, and constantly crying. Mitsuko was especially disappointed that Keiko-chan turned out to be a girl. Mitsuko asked if I remembered how bitter she was about Keiko-chan's birth, about motherhood. Indeed I did. After giving up on the thought of living on her own like her sister Izumi, of loving George, of having an exclusively self-centered life (she claimed to have been a *narushishisuto* [narcissist] at that time), she gradually resigned herself to her fate as a wife. But she was never the type simply to resign herself to anything. Once she decided to devote herself to her family, she became determined to be a success in the eyes of her parents. It was, therefore, important for her to have a male child. Giving birth to a son might mean that she would be the mother of someone who would be named successor in the Itoo household, someone who would eventually take over her father's enterprise. She realized that becoming pregnant, something that she had resisted for years, was really motivated by *yashin* (ambition).

She said that she had always been ambitious and had been proud of that personal characteristic, but becoming pregnant in order to be evaluated positively by her parents made her regret the existence of *yashin* in her. She was ashamed. At the time of her pregnancy, however, Mitsuko felt that everything had been taken away from her, her career, her independence, her passion, everything but her situation as a wife and her *chikara* (power) as a woman, that is, her ability to give birth. Given her emotional and social circumstances at the time of Keiko-chan's birth, it was natural for her, she said, to be deeply disappointed about giving birth to a girl. But a year later, she felt only regret and shame that something as pure and simple as childbirth could be so *kitanai* (dirty, sullied by ambition).

Now, Keiko-chan meant more to Mitsuko than what Mitsuko had initially intended her child to mean. Keiko-chan meant more than just a chance at the successorship in the Itoo household. Keiko-chan meant that Mitsuko could finally feel secure in her heart and mind. Keiko-chan was someone she could depend on in the future. If she had not had Keiko-chan and her parents died, there would be no one in the world to come to her aid. She really couldn't count on her friends, for in the final analysis, they were all *tanin*, outsiders. Keiko-chan would never be a *tanin*.

"What about your husband?" I asked.

Mitsuko replied that giving birth to Keiko-chan taught her a lot about human relationships. Keiko-chan, from the moment of birth, was involved in her *jinsei* (life, inner core of existence). The bond existed naturally. In part because their marriage had been arranged, she felt that that kind of bond with her husband had to be created, and when compared to her relationship with Keiko-chan, it was artificial. Her husband would always be a *tanin*.

In the year since Keiko-chan had come into her life, Mitsuko noticed a drastic change in her relationship with her husband. The violent arguments stopped. There was a growing tendency to lead separate lives. Although she was always there with him at public events, she no longer cared about where he spent his evenings or whether he came home at all. She no longer resented the secrets he kept from her. All she wanted to do was avoid conflict.

The constant battle between her and her husband, she supposed, came from her need to depend on someone. She was attempting to force a oneness, a wholeness, in her marriage. With Keiko-chan's birth, she discovered that she was one with another person—naturally. Mitsuko feared that she was becoming more and more involved in her child's existence. She feared that Keiko-chan would become the whole of her emotional life. But, Mitsuko thought, it might not be wrong to have fewer expectations of her husband. Perhaps, she reflected, it would be better to have less of an emotional commitment to her marriage. In any case, ever since Keiko-chan's arrival in the world, Mitsuko could claim an emotional state of peace, security, and even happiness.

After lunch, we looked at some dolls her father had ordered from a craftsman in Kyoto. They were intended for display at the Girls' Day Festival on March 3. We talked about who would be in attendance, and she said that she would be upset if Emiko, her sister-in-law, declined the invitation.

"Why would she do that?"

Mitsuko explained that Emiko and her older brother, still child-less, were envious of Mitsuko's favored position in their parents' household.

On March 3, Emiko was conspicuous by her absence. Mitsuko's older brother, who was present, made all the appropriate excuses.

Although Mitsuko regretted that *yashin* had been a motive for her pregnancy, she could not deny that such ambition is under-standable. Although the child's presence in her life meant more than just the gain of a competitive edge on her brothers and their wives for the household successorship, she did not deny that she enjoyed increased power and prestige because of the child. The ability to give birth proved to be an important, internally derived resource, which would advance her career within the household. Yet love was present.

The Meaning of Love

"In loving and being loved," Ann Swidler commented, "peo-ple give themselves over, at least for brief periods, to intensely moving experiences through which they achieve new awareness of self and others. Love can make possible periods of crystallization or reformulation of the self and the self's relationship to the world. Beliefs about love permeate people's hopes for themselves, their evaluations of experience, and their sense of achievement in the world."[8]

Ren'ai, the passionate love that Mitsuko Nishimura felt for George, left her breathless and afraid. According to Mitsuko, the deeper she fell in love, the more *sabishii* (lonely) she felt. Romantic love, although deeply moving, was, as she said, "mono tarinai" (lacking something). For her, there was no way to judge if love were really there. "In the final analysis," she told me, "I didn't know if I were being loved." There were no rules, no obligations, no points of reference. Romantic love was real, almost instinctive, but essentially shapeless. It left her feeling disconnected and unfulfilled.

Marriage pulled her out of her melancholia. But she resisted its pull for a long while, refusing to accept the presence of her husband by maintaining separate quarters although they shared the same residence. In the daily rhythms of life, however, shared by her and her husband, an emotional bond developed. They learned to love. "Well," she said, "in a way." At least they respected each other. He met his obligations as a husband. Yet she felt dissatisfied. She felt as if the relationship were based on *giri* alone. In her search for a oneness with her husband, she found only conflict. She realized that she was pushing too hard. Marriage, a social bond, was "artificial": its meaning derived almost entirely from societal expectations, from the structure of duties and obligations. Love in marriage, the meeting of society's expectations, was different from *ren'ai*, which was passionate, sexual, natural.

With the birth of her child and the development of parental love, the artificial and the natural, the societal and the instinctive, as Mitsuko understood the experience, became one. With the obligations between parent and child defined by society, the relationship had form and structure. Unlike the shapelessness of *ren'ai*, Mitsuko would know, definitely, that a bond between her and another existed. Unlike her marriage, which had been arranged and begun through structure alone, her love for Keiko-chan was motivated by something within her, something Mitsuko called *shizen* (natural). It was, for her, the completeness of experience that comes when *giri*, obligation, becomes *ninjoo*, a deep, inner sentiment. In parental love, Mitsuko felt secure and fulfilled perhaps for the first time in her adult life. At that crystalline moment when life began to make absolute sense, Mitsuko acquired a vocabulary of sentiments that would finally allow her to experience love—fully.[9]

"Authority discourages intimacy," George Homans and David Schneider once wrote.[10] Authority vested in the office is symbolically represented in the ideology of patrilineal descent, a line of men, not necessarily linked genetically, who have willingly given their lives to ensure the continued existence of the *ie* as a higher social order. Their actions and their power to organize the efforts of others in the household stem from their allegiance to the compulsory institution of the *ie*, thereby obtaining, without coercion, centralized control. The structure is hierarchical, a rigid ordering of positions within the corporate whole. The biological, the personal, the emotional, all that is intimate is suppressed, thereby guaranteeing the rational functioning of the *ie* as a perpetual social organization.

From a distance, the household seems populated with automatons, whose discharge of duties proceeds along lines both dispassionate and rational. The household seems, in fact, machine efficient and machine cold. The *ie* becomes a horrible vision out of Marcuse's *Eros and Civilization*, in which the individual, and all that is intimate, shrivels and dies in society's stranglehold.[11]

The *ie*—on the contrary—is nearly bursting with vengeance, passionate love, anger, ambition, nurturing care, envy, all of the exalted and sullied aspects of human nature and human emotion. The goings-on at the Moriuchis', the Okimotos', the Hayashis', and the Itoos' show us that social life is created precisely because passion, in all its human variety, exists. The individual's desire to influence the course of his or her own destiny, the need to love and be loved, sometimes desperate, are given form by, and, in turn, shape, the culture and social structure of the *ie*.[12]

NOTES

CHAPTER 1 BOUNDARIES

1. See Robert N. Bellah et al., *Habits of the Heart: Individualism and Commitment in American Life* (Berkeley, 1985). For a brilliantly executed and personal presentation of myths and their place in the life of immigrant America, see Maxine Hong Kingston, *The Woman Warrior: Memoirs of a Girlhood among Ghosts* (New York, 1976).

2. E.g., Ruth Benedict, *The Chrysanthemum and the Sword: Patterns of Japanese Culture* (Rutland, Vt., 1946).

3. Chie Nakane, *Japanese Society* (New York, 1973).

4. Ezra F. Vogel, *Japan as Number One: Lessons for America* (Cambridge, 1979).

5. S. N. Eisenstadt, *Revolution and the Transformation of Societies* (New York, 1978), pp. 1–45.

6. Pierre Bordieu, *Reproduction: In Education, Society, and Culture* (Beverly Hills, Calif., 1977).

7. Clifford Geertz, "Deep Play: Notes on the Balinese Cockfight," in *The Interpretation of Cultures: Selected Essays by Clifford Geertz* (New York, 1973), pp. 412–13.

8. By "blundering," I mean that hypotheses about human behavior in Japanese society, derived from my social scientific observations, were actually tested in the very actions that I took to establish myself as a person in a community; unfortunately, those hypotheses often proved to be dead wrong. Cf. Shulamit Reinharz, *On Becoming a Social Scientist* (San Francisco, 1979), p. 364.

9. Dorinne Kondo, "Dissolution and Reconstitution of Self: Implications for Anthropological Epistemology," *Cultural Anthropology*, 1 (February 1986), 76.

10. Nakane, *Japanese Society*, p. 20.

11. Helmut Morsbach, "Aspects of Nonverbal Communication in Japan," *Journal of Nervous and Mental Disease*, 157 (1973), 262.

12. Cf. Vincent Crapanzano, *Tuhami: Portrait of a Morroccan* (Chicago, 1980), p. 12.

13. Rosalie Wax, *Fieldwork: Warnings and Advice* (Chicago, 1971), p. 47.

14. For extremely insightful accounts of the experience of Japanese Americans in Japan, see Kondo, "Dissolution and Reconstitution of Self," pp. 74–88; and Daniel

I. Okimoto, *American in Disguise* (New York, 1971).

15. For an analysis of class-consciousness expressed in the meaning of objective behavior, see Susan A. Ostrander, "Upper-Class Women: Class Consciousness as Conduct and Meaning," in *Power Structure Research*, ed. G. William Domhoff (Beverly Hills, Calif., 1980), pp. 73–96.

16. For a detailed and excellent exposition of the concept *tatemae*, see Dorinne Kondo, "Work, Family and the Self: A Cultural Analysis of Japanese Family Enterprise" (Ph.D. diss., Harvard University, 1982), 45. Also see Roland Barthes, *Empire of Signs* (New York, 1982); and L. Takeo Doi, "*Omote* and *ura*: Concepts Derived from the Japanese Two-Fold Structure of Consciousness," *Journal of Nervous and Mental Disease*, 157 (1973), 258–61.

17. Cf. Emiko Ohnuki-Tierney, *Illness and Culture in Contemporary Japan* (Cambridge, 1984), pp. 21–50.

18. For an explication of shame as an emotive force in Japanese society, see Benedict, *Chrysanthemum and the Sword*.

19. Another variation in the usage of the personal pronoun *boku*: if the female is of the same age as the male, whom she addresses as *boku*, it implies a certain degree of possessiveness as well as intimacy; the relationship would, therefore, almost always be defined as a romantic attachment. For a more complete explication of first-person terms, see S. I. Harada, "Honorifics," in *Syntax and Semantics V: Japanese Generative Grammar*, ed. Masayoshi Shibatani (New York, 1976), pp. 499–561.

20. Shulamit Reinharz asked if downplaying my sexuality did not bring me ostracism and/or ridicule (personal communication, July 1985); and indeed, it did. Because I was not considered a mature adult, a real man as it were, by adult Japanese males, I was left in the company of women, who treated me as either a son or a younger brother. This left me open to ridicule by older males, culminating in their ostracism. As a result, my research began to focus, more and more, on the lives of women.

21. The problem of masking, of creating a new social identity in fieldwork, is addressed in Gerald D. Berreman, "Behind Many Masks: Ethnography and Impression Management in a Himalayan Village," in *Comparative Research Methods*, ed. Donald P. Warwick and Samuel Osherson (Englewood Cliffs, N.J., 1973), pp. 268–312.

22. Befu's study was first presented in Helmut Morsbach, "The Psychological Importance of Ritualized Gift Exchange in Modern Japan," in *Annals New York Academy of Sciences: Anthropology and the Climate of Opinion* (New York, 1977), p. 99.

23. Morsbach, "Ritualized Gift Exchange," p. 99.

24. Harumi Befu, *Japan: An Anthropological Introduction* (San Francisco, 1971), p. 169.

25. Ibid., p. 170.

26. Morsbach, "Ritualized Gift Exchange," pp. 100–101.

CHAPTER 2 PERSPECTIVES

1. See Jane Bachnik, "Inside and Outside the Japanese Household (*ie*): A Contextual Approach to Japanese Social Organization" (Ph.D. diss., Harvard University, 1978), 126.

2. I thank Scott C. McDonald, Director of Research, Time, Inc., for his critical insights into the study of the family. Our conversations about the study of the

family have been most useful.

3. Norman W. Bell and Ezra F. Vogel, "Toward a Framework for Functional Analysis of Family Behavior," in *The Family*, ed. Norman W. Bell and Ezra F. Vogel (New York, 1968), p. 3. See also Kiyomi Morioka, "Introduction: The Development of Family Sociology in Japan," *Journal of Comparative Family Studies*, 12 (1981), i–xiii.

4. Michelle Zimbalist Rosaldo, "Woman, Culture, and Society: A Theoretical Overview," in *Woman, Culture, and Society*, ed. Michelle Zimbalist Rosaldo and Louise Lamphere (Stanford, 1974), pp. 17–42.

5. Rosaldo, "Use and Abuse of Anthropology," pp. 408–9.

6. Sylvia Junko Yanagisako, "Family and Household: The Analysis of Domestic Groups," *Annual Review of Anthropology*, 8 (1979), 191.

7. Rosaldo, "Use and Abuse of Anthropology," p. 414. Yanagisako, "Family and Household," pp. 190–91.

CHAPTER 3 HOUSEHOLDS

1. Eldest-son succession is only a *preferred* strategy among many. Research on the Japanese family has often focused on the fact that such succession does not always occur. The debate, therefore, has often revolved around the contradiction between an ideal and a practice. See Harumi Befu, "Corporate Emphasis and Patterns of Descent in the Japanese Family," in *Japanese Culture: Its Development and Characteristics*, ed. Robert J. Smith and R. K. Beardsley (Chicago, 1962), pp. 34–41; and Keith Brown, "*Doozoku* and the Ideology of Descent in Rural Japan," *American Anthropologist*, 68 (1966), 1129–51. For an insightful analysis of that debate, see Laurel Cornell, "*Hajnal* and the Household in Asia: A Comparative History of the Family in Preindustrial Japan, 1600–1870," *Journal of Family History*, 12 (1987), 143–62.

The work of Laurel Cornell and Akira Hayami shows that primogeniture was not a fixed rule even in preindustrial Japan. Their work underscores the need to look at the household as more than a family unit, or a unit of biological reproduction. Their research on population registers of the Tokugawa period (1600–1868) shows that households operated beyond familial considerations. For example, when a household head retired, his record was changed to read "father." Clearly, authority rested not in the biological fact of fatherhood but in the position of household head. Furthermore, the notation "father" simply meant "the predecessor of the current household head"; that is, it could mean uncle, older brother, natural father, adopting father, father-in-law. See Laurel Cornell and Akira Hayami, "The *shuumon aratame choo*: Japan's Population Registers," *Journal of Family History*, 11 (1986), 311–28; and Laurel Cornell, "Retirement, Inheritance, and Intergenerational Conflict in Preindustrial Japan," *Journal of Family History*, 8 (1983), 55–69.

In his investigation of the Tokugawa population registers, Robert J. Smith emphasized the importance of movement, of decision making. He defined the household as a process, as well as a structure, in which constantly developing combinations of individuals could be grouped so that the continuity of the social organization of the household could be assured. "The Domestic Cycle in Selected Commoner Families in Urban Japan, 1757–1858," *Journal of Family History*, 3 (1978), 219–35. The Meiji Civil Code of 1898 embodied this blend of structure and process-in-choice. In an extremely insightful analysis, Jane Bachnik noted that "the Meiji Code is very widely cited as legislating succession by a 'rule' of 'primogeniture,' and its influence has been widespread, even at the popular level. But the code itself mentions neither the term translated as 'primogeniture' (*chooshi* or *choonan soozoku*), nor any 'rule' of succession. Succession is presented as a series of five rankings for sets of features which are given in the following order: near/far; male/female; legitimate/illegitimate; gender vs. legitimacy; and older/younger (*Minpoo* [The Meiji Civil Code], Article 970). Both the relation between the features and that between *sets* of features are legislated in the code. If the preferred feature is selected in each of the five sets, and the ranking is followed between the sets, the outcome is the 'nearest' 'relative,' who is also 'male,' 'legitimate,' and 'eldest.' But this is not a 'rule,' because *the choice is not stipulated*. The relationships between all the other features are included in this (and all the choices), and all the other permutations of the choices are acceptable. The components of the possible choices are presented, and preferences between the features. But the code does not stipulate how to make the choice. An entire system has been legislated in the rankings. Furthermore, 'adoptive' persons are allowed the same status as legitimate children, which means that an adoptee can be included in the same ranking of features (and conceivably can be defined as 'nearest,' 'male,' 'legitimate,' and 'eldest')." "Recruitment Strategies for Household Succession: Rethinking Japanese Household Organisation," *Man*, 18 (1983), 169.

By codifying only a preference for primogeniture, the Meiji Civil Code, in fact, allowed for continued flexibility in the ability of the *ie* to recruit competent leadership; and by not stipulating the necessity of blood ties in the matter of succession, the *ie* remained free of the restriction of kinship.

2. John C. Pelzel, "Japanese Kinship: A Comparison," in *Family and Kinship in Chinese Society*, ed. Maurice Freedman (Stanford, 1970), p. 235. "The thesis that the 'lineage' is in function more a community than a kinship organization is perfectly true, but this organization is not necessarily limited to a single territorial community, nor does it perform functions that are necessarily seen to be of community wide use. Since it is always based on unequal distribution of power resources it seems appropriate to suggest that 'lineage' is primarily an instrument for the organization of power. Its functions seem usually to involve gaining power advantages not otherwise procurable by the members of a hierarchically organized community. For the senior member, a 'lineage' means dependable labor and support to be worked by the household alone. For the junior member it means the assured use of capital goods he does not himself own, and a role he would not otherwise acquire in communal affairs controlled by others" (p. 236). See also John C. Pelzel, "The Small Industrialist in Japan," in *Explorations in Entrepreneurial History*, ed. Aitken (Cambridge, 1965), pp. 79–93; Edward Norbeck and Harumi Befu, "Informal Fictive Kinship in Japan," *American Anthropologist*, 60 (1958), 102–12; Iwao Ishino, "The *oyabun-kobun*: A Japanese Ritual Kinship Institution," *American Anthropologist*, 55 (1953), 695–707; and Harumi Befu, "Ritual Kinship in Japan: Its Variability and Resiliency," *Sociologus*, 14 (1963), 150–69.

The concept of the *ie* was used by both government and business to quell labor and political unrest in Japan's early industrial period. See M. Y. Yoshino, *Japan's Managerial System: Tradition and Innovation* (Cambridge, 1968); and Fruin, *Kikkoman*, pp. 211–25. For an analysis of the development of working-class consciousness in early industrial Japan, see Andrew Gordon, *The Evolution of Labor Relations in Japan: Heavy Industry, 1853–1955* (Cambridge, 1985). For women's involvement in the early labor movement, see Sharon Sievers, *Flowers in Salt: The Beginnings of the Feminist Consciousness in Modern Japan* (Stanford, 1983); and E. Patricia Tsurumi, "Female

Textile Workers and the Failure of Early Trade Unionism in Japan," *History Workshop Journal*, 18 (1984), 3–27.

3. Hironobu Kitaoji, "The Structure of the Japanese Family," *American Anthropologist*, 73 (1971), 1048.

4. Bachnik, "Recruitment Strategies for Household Succession," p. 167.

5. If scholars fail to recognize the formal regularity of the *ie* as a positional organization and when they strictly define the *ie* as a familial unit that operates on the basis of patrilineal descent, patrilocal residence, and primogeniture, they will find a bewildering array of familial forms, but this should not serve as the basis of an argument that the *ie* does not and did not exist as a sociocentric organization. I would suggest that they may have come across a variety of strategies that would ensure the survival of the *ie* as a corporate group and that the array of strategies probably fits within the formal regularities of the *ie*. For the array of familial practices in historical and contemporary perspectives, see Kazuo Ueno, "Daikazoku, kokazoku, chokkeikazoku: Nihon no kazoku kenkyuu no mittsu no keifu," *Shakaijinruigaku Nenpoo*, 10 (1984), 40–43; Michio Suenari, "First Child Inheritance in Japan," *Ethnology*, 11 (1972), 122–26; Yuujiro Ooguchi, "Kinsei kooki ni okeru nooson kazoku no keitai: Josei soozokujin o chuushin ni," in *Nihon josei shi, III: Kinsei* (Tokyo, 1982), pp. 202–11: Takeyoshi Kawashima, *Nihon shakai no kazokuteki koosei* (Tokyo, 1948), pp. 11–15; Kunio Yanagida, *Japanese Manners and Customs in the Meiji Era* (Tokyo, 1957), pp. 161–68; Takashi Koyama, *The Changing Social Position of Women in Japan* (Geneva, 1961), p. 87; and Michiko Miyashita, "Nooson ni okeru kazoku kon-in," in *Nihon josei shi, III: Kinsei* (Tokyo, 1982), pp. 61–62.

6. For women, the *tekireiki* period is from the age of twenty to twenty-seven, after which a woman may be regarded as a *hai missu* (a term derived from English *high* and *miss* and incorporated into contemporary Japanese to mean *spinster*). For men, the *tekireiki* period begins at the age of twenty-five and extends to about thirty-one.

7. Sooichiro Tahara also noted that it was common for daughters of men who are listed in the *Shinshiroku* (The Gentlemen's Directory, or Social Registry), to marry those whom Tahara called *"Toodai de shomin"* (commoner graduates of Tokyo University). *Nihon no pawaa eriito* (Tokyo, 1980), pp. 175–88.

8. By referring to himself as *shachoo* (president) instead of *Papa* (Papa) or *Otoosan* (Father), he was clearly pulling rank, invoking his authority as the household head as well as president of the household enterprise.

9. For an extremely insightful analysis of the notion of person, and its communication, in Japanese society, see Jane Bachnik, "Deixis and Self/Other Reference in Japanese Discourse," *Working Papers in Sociolinguistics*, 99 (July 1982), 1–36.

10. Kondo, "Work, Family, and the Self," pp. 102–3.

11. Nakane, *Japanese Society*, p. 5.

12. Samuel E. Martin, "Speech Levels in Japan and Korea," in *Language in Culture and Society*, ed. Dell Hymes (New York, 1964), p. 409.

13. David M. Schneider, "What Is Kinship All About?" in *Kinship Studies in the Morgan Centennial Year*, ed. Priscilla Reining (Washington, D.C., 1972), p. 38.

14. Bachnik suggested that in terms of self/other relationships, "The focus in English is on the ends of the continuum (and on subjectivity and objectivity) rather than on the continuum itself; the focus in Japanese is on the continuum itself, rather than the poles. But if the continuum in Japanese discourse is compared with the Indo-European discourse *poles*, the result is an 'open-ended' or 'variable' *self*." "Deixis and Self/Other Reference," pp. 26–27.

15. For a detailed and elegant explication of the *yamanote/shitamachi* opposition, see Kondo, "Work, Family, and the Self," pp. 83–91.

16. Bachnik, "Inside and Outside the Japanese Household," p. 146.

17. Kondo, "Work, Family, and the Self."

CHAPTER 4 DEATH

1. Nobushige Hozumi, *Ancestor Worship and Japanese Law*, 6th ed. (Tokyo,1940), pp. 17–18.

2. Ibid., pp. 18–19.

3. For an excellent explication of the tendency to embody physically psychological phenomena in Japanese culture, see Ohnuki-Tierney, *Illness and Culture in Contemporary Japan*, pp. 75–88. About indigenous forms of psychotherapy, see David K. Reynolds, *The Quiet Therapies: Japanese Pathways to Personal Growth* (Honolulu, 1980).

4. The sleeve guard is a flexible wicker tube that fits over the forearm. It keeps the kimono sleeve from sticking to the skin in the summer humidity.

5. Bachnik, "Inside and Outside the Japanese Household," p. 90.

6. In regions outside Tokyo, *obon* occurs between August 13 and 16.

7. Herman Ooms, "A Structural Analysis of Japanese Ancestral Rites and Beliefs," in *Ancestors*, ed. William H. Newell (Chicago, 1976), p. 67. David W. Plath, "Where the Family of God Is the Family: The Role of the Dead in Japanese Households," *American Anthropologist*, 66 (1964), 300–317. Robert J. Smith, *Ancestor Worship in Contemporary Japan* (Stanford, 1974), p. 57.

8. Ibid.

9. Ooms, "Japanese Ancestral Rites and Beliefs," pp. 67–68.

10. This is standard practice in Japanese funerary rites.

11. Note, however, that this kind of referring and addressing by the use of positional kinship terms is used only when a status subordinate addresses or refers to a status superior. For example, an older sister would not address a younger brother by the positional kinship term of *otooto* (Younger Brother), but by his given name instead. Whereas, the younger brother is enjoined to address his older sister as *oneesama* (Older Sister or Big Sister).

12. All members of the household are in mourning until the forty-ninth day; however, especially close members may choose to remain in mourning until the hundredth day.

13. Ooms, "Japanese Ancestral Rites and Beliefs," pp. 67-68.

14. R. J. Smith, *Ancestor Worship in Contemporary Japan*, p. 20.

15. The posthumous name of the deceased and the name of the person(s) who commissioned the writing of the *otooba* are written on the slats. They are placed on the grave on periodic deathday anniversaries or seasonal events, such as *obon* or the equinoxes. In some areas, the size of the *otooba* changes, getting larger with each commemorative event. In other areas, the size remains the same but a different inscription is written for each event. *Otooba* are commissioned until the last commemorative event for the deceased, which is either the thirty-third or fiftieth deathday anniversary.

16. Herman Ooms, "The Religion of the Household: A Case Study of Ancestor Worship in Japan," *Contemporary Religions in Japan*, 8 (1967), 240.

17. Plath, "Where the Family of God Is the Family," p. 304.

18. Ooms pointed out that it is not necessarily the case that an *ihai* would not be written for a child or an unmarried adult in death: a full-fledged wooden *ihai* may be commissioned. It is also just as probable that only a temporary one in paper for the funeral services will be made. "Japanese Ancestral Rites and Beliefs," p. 69.

19. Ibid.

20. Plath, "Where the Family of God Is the Family," pp. 300–317.

21. Ooms, "Japanese Ancestral Rites and Beliefs," p. 66.

22. Plath, "Where the Family of God Is the Family," p. 303.

23. R. J. Smith, *Ancestor Worship in Contemporary Japan*, p. 123. Emphasis added.

24. Plath, "Where the Family of God Is the Family," p. 312. *Me and You* (Tokyo, 1962).

25. R. J. Smith, *Ancestor Worship in Contemporary Japan*, pp. 133–34.

26. Ooms, "Religion of the Household," p. 298.

27. Ibid., p. 300.

28. Negative behavior is also defined, for as Robert J. Smith pointed out, "death does not wipe out memories of enmity and conflict." *Ancestor Worship in Contemporary Japan*, p. 115.

CHAPTER 5 AUTHORITY

1. See Pelzel, "Japanese Kinship," pp. 235–36.

2. Keith Brown, "The Content of *doozoku* Relationships in Japan," *Ethnology*, 7 (1968), 118–19.

3. Nakane, *Japanese Society*, p. 45.

4. Ibid., p. 49.

5. Pelzel, "Japanese Kinship," pp. 233–39.

6. Personal communication, March 1982. There is also the possibility of downward mobility if a family is established as a branch family. For a historical study of branching and mobility, see Akira Hayami, "Labor Migration in a Pre-Industrial Society: A Study Tracing the Life Histories of the Inhabitants of a Village," *Keio Economic Studies*, 10 (1973), 1–17, especially pp. 16–17.

7. Michel Crozier, *The Bureaucratic Phenomenon* (Chicago, 1964), pp. 187–88.

8. Max Weber, "The Social Psychology of World Religions," in *From Max Weber: Essays in Sociology*, ed. and trans. H. H. Gerth and C. Wright Mills (New York, 1974), p. 294.

9. Max Weber, "Bureaucracy," in *From Max Weber: Essays in Sociology*, ed. and trans. H. H. Gerth and C. Wright Mills (New York, 1974), p. 228.

10. Crozier, *Bureaucratic Phenomenon*, p. 158.

11. Brown, "Content of *doozoku* Relationships," p. 121.

12. For further details on *inkyo bunke*, see ibid.

13. For further details about intrahousehold conflict at the time of succession, see Keith Brown and Michio Suenari, "Bunke no bunshutsu ni tsuite," *Minzokugaku Kenkyuu*, 31 (1966), 38–48.

14. Rosabeth Moss Kanter, *Men and Women of the Corporation* (New York, 1977), p. 171.

15. Ibid.

16. James D. Thompson, *Organizations in Action* (New York, 1967), p. 125.

17. Ibid.

18. Ibid., p. 126.

19. For a fascinating explication of fiduciary relationships in business families, see George E. Marcus, "The Fiduciary Role in American Family Dynasties and Their Institutional Legacy: From the Law of Trusts to Trust in the Establishment," in *Elites: Ethnographic Issues*, ed. George E. Marcus (Albuquerque, 1983), pp. 221–56.

20. Kantoo Investment Counsellors, Limited, seems similar to the kind of "family office" found among upper-class American families, about which Marvin G. Dunn wrote: "Internal coordination manifests itself through the strengthening of kinship bonds between family members. This is accomplished by the office in its management of trusts and foundations. Both trusts and foundations have stock portfolios that enable the office to provide links between the generations and to link different nuclear units of the larger kin group together. In addition to common economic interests (joint stock holdings), trusts and foundations provide added linkages through shared trusteeships and common foundation boards. Internal coordination thus serves to strengthen family cohesiveness." "The Family Office: Coordinating Mechanism of the Ruling Class," in *Power Structure Research*, ed. G. William Domhoff (Beverly Hills, Calif., 1980), p. 43.

21. In addition to the *butsudan*, these properties are also sacred, concrete embodiments of household tradition. George E. Marcus remarked that "such assets can be passed on by bequest or grabbing in a subsequent generation, but any attempt to liquidate them generally causes bitter internal disputes. . . . In the aging of dynasties, the desacralization of such objects can occur gradually, alienated by persons who become marginal participants in dynastic affairs, or spectacularly through the effort of a descendant to sell commercially valuable sacred assets and the opposition that this arouses in others. Either the willingness or need to desacralize objects by alienation is one salient index, among others, of a stage in the dissolving organization of a dynasty." "Spending," p. 238.

CHAPTER 6 MARRIAGE

1. Ezra F. Vogel, "The Go-Between in a Developing Society: The Case of the Japanese Marriage Arranger," *Human Organization*, 20 (Fall 1961), 119–20.

A *nakoodo* could be either male or female and is usually someone who carries out the responsibility of *endan o tsukuru* (making a match) on an informal basis. In fact, it is said that one should make three matches in one's life after one has gotten married. There are, however, semiprofessional and professional matchmakers, whose personal incomes are substantially bolstered by the gift money involved.

2. About marriage and its effect on household status, Chie Nakane wrote, "In order to raise the status of a household, outstanding economic achievement is not sufficient; increased status can only be recognized socially through *engumi* [affinal links]. For a rising household with great economic success to enter into marriage with a household of higher status signifies social recognition, and so confers the deserved increased status. On the other hand, to marry into a household of considerably lower status implies a lowering of one's own status, and this lowering embraces the other households of one's network." *Kinship and Economic Organization in Rural Japan* (New York, 1967), p. 158. Although Nakane's remarks pertain to a rural community, I was struck by the similarity of concerns about marriage among my informant households, which in essence, made up a close-knit community, a "village" encompassing wealthy households, centered in Tokyo.

3. E. F. Vogel, "Go-Between in a Developing Society," pp. 114, 116.

4. For an analysis of relationships of dependency in Japan, see Hisa A. Kumagai, "A Dissection of Intimacy: A Study of 'Bipolar Posturing' in Japanese Social Interaction—*amaeru* and *amayakasu*, Indulgence and Deference," *Culture, Medicine, and Psychiatry*, 5 (1981), 249–72.

5. Nakane, *Kinship and Economic Organization*, pp. 152–53.

6. Ibid, p. 153.

7. Mrs. Okimoto would agree with James M. Ault, Jr., who wrote, "The capacity of gossip to alter reputations in a public realm represents a power that transcends both the actual conduct of individuals and the private beliefs others have of them and their conduct. It is deployed, then, within a definite political space. In communities where it looms large as a pervasive social reality, it is its inescapable political, rather than simply moral, dimension that compels individual members to remain active in its circuitry, or risk the consequences." "Class Differences in Family Structure and the Social Bases of Modern Feminism" (Ph.D. diss., Brandeis University, 1981), 348–49.

8. For an excellent interpretation of the concepts of *tatemae* and *honne*, see Kondo, "Work, Family, and the Self," pp. 45–46.

9. About the dangers of trading information among informants, see Arlene Kaplan Daniels, "The Low-Caste Stranger in Social Research," in *Ethics, Politics, and Social Research*, ed. Gideon Sjoberg (Cambridge, 1967), pp. 267–96; Arlene Kaplan Daniels, "Self-Deception and Self-Discovery in Fieldwork," *Qualitative Sociology*, 6 (1983), 195–214; and Paul Rabinow, *Reflections on Fieldwork in Morocco* (Berkeley, 1977).

10. As Jane Bachnik wrote: "I must stress that this is not a single network, but a multiple series of semi-overlapping ones. Each household is a social context with its own focal point. Thus each is its own focal point. Thus each its own '0-Point' set for its system of relationship coordinates, and each time one moves a step from a household, the perspective changes so that *that* house is the new focal point. Strictly speaking, there are no two-step links, but only a series of overlapping one-step links, which one moves along." "Inside and Outside the Japanese Household," pp. 138–39.

11. Chie Nakane wrote: "A wealthy household tends to have a broader range of *shinrui* [or *shinseki*], while the poorer sector of the community tends to have a narrower range. When members of *shinrui* reside far apart, they easily cease to interact, yet a wealthy household will maintain contact with quite distant *shinrui*. The maintenance of the *shinrui* relationships thus tends to depend largely upon the location of a household and its economic standing.

Shinrui is determined not only by the recognition of kinship distance, but also by the performance of duties and obligations between households. Failure of the latter often leads to termination of the relationship, whatever be the actual kinship recognized." *Kinship and Economic Organization*, pp. 35–36.

12. Nakane, *Kinship and Economic Organization*, p. 31. Jane Bachnik presents the process of "fading" in detail. See Bachnik, "Inside and Outside the Japanese Household," pp. 124–25.

13. Bachnik, p. 126. The research of Sylvia Junko Yanagisako among Japanese Americans suggests that women may be allowed to move freely between households because of their culturally constructed occupation with the emotional aspects of life; and since emotion is not seen by men, heads of households, as threatening to jural and economic autonomy, women play an important role in developing linkages between households. "A woman's solidary ties," Yanagisako notes, "and her con-

sequent ability to mobilize people, are an important resource both for herself and for members of her family." "Women-centered Kin Networks in Urban Bilateral Kinship," *American Ethnologist,* 4 (1977), 207–26.

CHAPTER 7 LOVE

1. Takie Sugiyama Lebra observed that this tie between mother and daughter serves as a social "buffer" for the new bride. *Japanese Women: Constraint and Fulfillment* (Honolulu, 1984), pp. 151–52.

2. Nakane, *Kinship and Economic Organization,* p. 23. For further observations of this phenomenon, see Ronald P. Dore, *Shinohata: A Portrait of a Japanese Village* (New York, 1978), p. 145.

3. For an analysis of a similar situation in the Taiwanese household, see Margery Wolf, *Women and the Family in Rural Taiwan* (Stanford, 1972).

4. The importance of *shinseki* relationships was underscored by Harumi Befu, who remarked that these "ties of kinship provide Japan a network of relationships which resolves recurrent problems in the spheres of economic assistance . . . and expressive solidarity." "Patrilineal Descent and Personal Kindred in Japan," *American Anthropologist,* 65 (December 1963), 1333.

5. About the factors that influence the bride's successful change in status, Nakane wrote: "The structure of the household produces a sociological weakness in the wife's initial position. But when she succeeds to a secure position as the mistress of the household she usually has the chance to overcome her handicap as a wife, and thus are the power and influence of women discreetly maintained in Japanese society. Further, as in the case of the father, actual economic contribution also gives an advantageous position to the wife: her labour can be important in the household economy, or she may have brought substantial property at her marriage. It is extremely difficult to describe *the* status (in the sense of power and prestige) of Japanese women in the household. It can be very low, or very high—it all depends on the situation in which she is involved. The following factors have to be taken into account: her status in the household (whether she is the mistress or not); the degree of her economic contribution to the household; the degree to which status differentiations in the household are institutionalized; the economic situation of the household she has entered, as well as that from which she came; competing personal relationships among the household members; her character, personality and ability; local customs; the ideology prevailing at a given time. The complex of all these factors determines her actual power and prestige in the household." Nakane, *Kinship and Economic Organization,* p. 25.

6. Brown, *"Doozoku* and the Ideology of Descent," pp. 1143–44.

7. Ibid., p. 1144.

8. Ann Swidler, "Love and Adulthood in American Culture," in *Themes of Work and Love in Adulthood,* ed. Neil J. Smelser and Erik H. Erikson (Cambridge, 1980), p. 121.

9. See Steven L. Gordon, "The Sociology of Sentiments and Emotion," in *Social Psychology: Sociological Perspectives,* ed. Morris Rosenberg and Ralph H. Turner (New York, 1981), p. 563.

"Not until one bears a child," Takie Sugiyama Lebra was told, "can one truly understand the essence of human love or empathize with human beings." *Japanese Women,* p. 165. To interpret that statement, as well as Mitsuko's experience, we must consider Margery Wolf's essential point that the worldview of women is tied to their structural positions within households. See her *Women and the Family in Rural Taiwan* (Stanford, 1972).

10. George C. Homans and David M. Schneider, *Marriage, Authority, and Final Causes: A Study of Unilateral Cross-Cousin Marriages* (Glencoe, Ill., 1955), p. 58.

11. Herbert Marcuse, *Eros and Civilization* (New York, 1955).

12. "Bursts of feeling," commented Michelle Zimbalist Rosaldo, "will continue to be opposed to careful thought. But recognition of the fact that thought is always culturally patterned and infused with feeling . . . suggests that just as thought does not exist in isolation from affective life, so affect is culturally ordered and does not exist apart from thought." "Toward an Anthropology of Self and Feeling," in *Culture Theory: Essays on Mind, Self, and Emotion*, ed. Richard A. Shweder and Robert A. LeVine (Cambridge, 1984), p. 137.

BIBLIOGRAPHY

Althusser, Louis. "Ideology and Ideological State Apparatuses." In *Lenin and Philosophy*, edited and translated by Ben Brewster, 27–86. New York: Monthly Review Press, 1971.

Ariga, Kizaemon, Takashi Nakano, Kiyomi Morioka, and John S. Morton. "The Japanese Family." Typescript, Tookyoo Kyooiku Daigaku, January 1953.

Ault, James M., Jr. "Class Differences in Family Structure and the Social Bases of Modern Feminism." Ph.D. diss., Department of Sociology, Brandeis University, 1981.

Bachnik, Jane. "Deixis and Self/Other Reference in Japanese Discourse." *Working Papers in Sociolinguistics*, 99 (July 1982), 1–36.

———. "Inside and Outside the Japanese Household (*ie*): A Contextual Approach to Japanese Social Organization." Ph.D. diss., Department of Anthropology, Harvard University, 1978.

———. "Recruitment Strategies for Household Succession: Rethinking Japanese Household Organisation." *Man*, 18 (1983), 160–82.

Baltzell, E. Digby. *The Protestant Establishment*. New York: Vintage, 1964.

Barthes, Roland. *Empire of Signs*. New York: Wang and Hill, 1982.

Becker, Howard S. "Art as Collective Action." *American Sociological Review*, 33 (December 1974), 767–76.

Befu, Harumi. "Corporate Emphasis and Patterns of Descent in the Japanese Family." In *Japanese Culture: Its Development and Characteristics*, edited by Robert J. Smith and R. K. Beardsley, 34–41. Chicago: Aldine, 1962.

———. "Ecology, Residence, and Authority: The Corporate Household in Central Japan." *Ethnology*, 7 (1969), 25–42.

———. "Gift-Giving in a Modernizing Japan." *Monumenta Nipponica*, 23 (1968), 445–56.

———. *Japan: An Anthropological Introduction*. San Francisco: Chandler, 1971.

————. "Patrilineal Descent and Personal Kindred in Japan." *American Anthropologist*, 65 (December 1963), 1328–41.

————. "Ritual Kinship in Japan: Its Variability and Resiliency." *Sociologus*, 14 (1963), 150–69.

Bell, Norman W., and Ezra F. Vogel. "Toward a Framework for Functional Analysis of Family Behavior." In *The Family*, edited by Norman W. Bell and Ezra F. Vogel, 1–34. New York: Free Press, 1968.

Bellah, Robert N. "Religious Evolution." *American Sociological Review*, 29 (1964) 358–74.

Bellah, Robert N., Richard Madsen, William M. Sullivan, Ann Swidler, and Steven M. Tipton. *Habits of the Heart: Individualism and Commitment in American Life.* Berkeley: University of California Press, 1985.

Bendix, Reinhard. *Work and Authority in Industry: Ideologies of Management in the Course of Industrialization.* Berkeley: University of California Press, 1974.

Benedict, Ruth. *The Chrysanthemum and the Sword: Patterns of Japanese Culture.* Rutland, Vt.: Charles E. Tuttle, 1946.

Berreman, Gerald D. "Behind Many Masks: Ethnography and Impression Management in a Himalayan Village." In *Comparative Research Methods*, edited by Donald P. Warwick and Samuel Osherson, 263–312. Englewood Cliffs, N.J.: Prentice-Hall, 1973.

Blood, Robert O., Jr. *Love Match and Arranged Marriage: A Tokyo-Detroit Comparison.* New York: Free Press, 1977.

Bordieu, Pierre. *Reproduction: In Education, Society, and Culture.* Beverly Hills, Calif.: Sage Publications, 1977.

Bott, Elizabeth. *Family and Social Network.* New York: Free Press, 1971.

Brown, Keith. "The Content of *doozoku* Relationships in Japan." *Ethnology*, 7 (1968), 113–39.

————. "*Doozoku* and the Ideology of Descent in Rural Japan." *American Anthropologist*, 68 (1966), 1129–51.

Brown, Keith, and Michio Suenari. "Bunke no bunshutsu ni tsuite." *Minzokugaku kenkyuu*, 31 (1966), 38–48.

Caudill, William A. "The Influence of Social Structure and Culture on Human Behavior in Modern Japan." *Journal of Nervous and Mental Disease*, 157 (1973), 240–57.

Coleman, Samuel. "The Tempo of Family Formation." In *Work and Lifecourse in Japan*, edited by David W. Plath, 183–214. Albany: State University of New York Press, 1983.

Collier, Jane F., and Michelle Z. Rosaldo. "Politics and Gender in Simple Societies." In *Sexual Meanings: The Cultural Construction of Gender and Sexuality*, edited by Sherry B. Ortner and Harriet Whitehead, 275–329. Cambridge: Cambridge University Press, 1981.

Collins, Randall. "On the Microfoundations of Macrosociology." *American Journal of Sociology*, 86 (1981), 984–1014.

Cook, Alice H., and Hiroko Hayashi. *Working Women in Japan: Discrimination, Resistance, and Reform.* Ithaca: New York State School of Industrial and Labor Relations Press, 1980.

176

Cornell, Laurel. "*Hajnal* and the Household in Asia: A Comparative History of the Family in Preindustrial Japan, 1600–1870." *Journal of Family History*, 12 (1987), 143–62.

———. "Retirement, Inheritance, and Intergenerational Conflict in Preindustrial Japan." *Journal of Family History*, 8 (1983), 55–69.

———. "Why Are There No Spinsters in Japan?" *Journal of Family History*, 9 (1984), 326–39.

Cornell, Laurel, and Akira Hayami. "The *shuumon aratame choo*: Japan's Population Registers." *Journal of Family History*, 11 (1986), 311–28.

Crapanzano, Vincent. *Tuhami: Portrait of a Moroccan*. Chicago: University of Chicago Press, 1980.

Crozier, Michel. *The Bureaucratic Phenomenon*. Chicago: University of Chicago Press, 1964.

Cummings, William K. *Education and Equality in Japan*. Princeton: Princeton University Press, 1980.

Daniels, Arlene Kaplan. "The Low-Caste Stranger in Social Research." In *Ethics, Politics, and Social Research*, edited by Gideon Sjoberg, 267–96. Cambridge, Mass.: Schenkman, 1967.

———. "Self-Deception and Self-Discovery in Fieldwork." *Qualitative Sociology*, 6 (1983), 195–214.

Devereaux, George. *From Anxiety to Method in the Behavioral Sciences*. The Hague, Netherlands: Mouton, 1967.

DeVos, George, and Hiroshi Wagatsuma, eds. *Japan's Invisible Race*. Berkeley: University of California Press, 1966.

di Leonardo, Micaela. *The Varieties of Ethnic Experience: Kinship, Class, and Gender among California Italian-Americans*. Ithaca, N.Y.: Cornell University Press, 1984.

DiMaggio, Paul. "Cultural Capital and School Success: The Impact of Status Culture Participation on the Grades of U.S. High School Students." *American Sociological Review*, 47 (1982), 189–201.

DiMaggio, Paul, and John Mohr. "Cultural Capital, Educational Attainment, and Marital Selection." *American Journal of Sociology*, 90 (1985), 1231–61.

DiTomaso, Nancy. "Organizational Analysis and Power Structure Research." In *Power Structure Research*, edited by G. William Domhoff, 255–68. Beverly Hills, Calif.: Sage Publications, 1980.

Doi, L. Takeo. "*Omote* and *ura*: Concepts Derived from the Japanese Two-Fold Structure of Consciousness." *Journal of Nervous and Mental Disease*, 157 (1973), 258–61.

Domhoff, G. William. *The Higher Circles: The Governing Class in America*. New York: Random House, 1970.

———. *Who Rules America Now? A View for the '80s*. Englewood Cliffs, N.J.: Prentice-Hall, 1983.

Dore, Ronald P. *Shinohata: A Portrait of a Japanese Village*. New York: Pantheon Books, 1978.

Duncan, Hugh D. "Literature as Equipment for Action: Burke's Dramatistic Conception." In *The Sociology of Art and Literature*, edited by Milton C. Albrecht, James H. Barnett, and Mason Griff, 713–23. New York: Praeger, 1970.

Dunn, Marvin G. "The Family Office: Coordinating Mechanism of the Ruling Class." In *Power Structure Research*, edited by G. William Domhoff, 8–45. Beverly Hills, Calif: Sage Publications, 1980.

Eisenstadt, S. N. *Revolution and the Transformation of Societies*. New York: Free Press, 1978.

Elson, Diane, and Ruth Pierson. "The Subordination of Women and the Internationalization of Factory Production." In *Of Marriage and the Market: Women's Subordination Internationally and Its Lessons*, edited by Kate Young, Carol Walkowitz, and Roslyn McCullagh, 18–40. London: Routledge, Kegan, and Paul, 1981.

Farley, Jennie. *Women Workers in Fifteen Countries*. Ithaca: New York State School of Industrial and Labor Relations Press, 1985.

Fruin, W. Mark. *Kikkoman: Company, Clan, and Community*. Cambridge: Harvard University Press, 1983.

Fuse, Akiko. "The Japanese Family in Transition." *Japan Foundation Newsletter*, 12 (1984), 1–11.

Geertz, Clifford. "Deep Play: Notes on the Balinese Cockfight." In *The Interpretation of Cultures: Selected Essays by Clifford Geertz*, 412–53. New York: Basic Books, 1973.

———. "Ethos, World View, and the Analysis of Sacred Symbols." In *The Interpretation of Cultures: Selected Essays by Clifford Geertz*, 126–41. New York: Basic Books, 1973.

———. *Islam Observed: Religious Development in Morocco and Indonesia*. Chicago: University of Chicago Press, 1968.

Gombrich, Ernst Hans. *Art and Illusion*. New York: Pantheon Books, 1960.

Gordon, Andrew. *The Evolution of Labor Relations in Japan: Heavy Industry, 1853–1955*. Cambridge: Harvard University Press, 1985.

Gordon, Steven L. "The Sociology of Sentiments and Emotion." In *Social Psychology: Sociological Perspectives*, edited by Morris Rosenberg and Ralph H. Turner, 562–92. New York: Basic Books, 1981.

Hansen, Edward C., and Timothy C. Parrish. "Elites versus the State: Toward an Anthropological Contribution to the Study of Hegemonic Power in Capitalist Society." In *Elites: Ethnographic Issues*, edited by George E. Marcus, 257–77. Albuquerque: University of New Mexico Press, 1983.

Harada, S. I. "Honorifics." In *Syntax and Semantics V: Japanese Generative Grammar*, edited by Masayoshi Shibatani, 499–561. New York: Academic Press, 1976.

Hashimoto, Akiko. "Roojin Care no Nichibei haikaku: Odawarashi to West Haven." *Kazoku: shakai to hoo*, 1 (1985), 40–51.

Hayami, Akira. "Class Differences in Marriage and Fertility among Tokugawa Villagers in Mino Province." *Keio Economic Studies*, 17 (1980), 1–16.

———. "Labor Migration in a Pre-Industrial Society: A Study Tracing the Life Histories of the Inhabitants of a Village." *Keio Economic Studies*, 10 (1973), 1–17.

———. "The Myth of Primogeniture and Impartible Inheritance in Tokugawa Japan." *Journal of Family History*, 8 (1983) 3–29.

Hayami, Akira, and Nobuko Uchida. "Size of Household in a Japanese County throughout the Tokugawa Era." In *Household and Family in Past Time*, edited by Peter Laslett, 473–515. Cambridge: Cambridge University Press, 1972.

Hendry, Joy. *Marriage in Changing Japan: Community and Society*. London: Croom Helm, 1981.

Hochschild, Arlie Russell. *The Managed Heart: Commercialization of Human Feeling*. Berkeley: University of California Press, 1983.

Homans, George C., and David M. Schneider. *Marriage, Authority, and Final Causes: A Study of Unilateral Cross-Cousin Marriages*. Glencoe, Ill.: Free Press, 1955.

Hozumi, Nobushige. *Ancestor Worship and Japanese Law*. 6th ed. Tokyo: Hokuseido Press, 1940.

Huerta, Faye C., and Thomas A. Lane. "Participation of Women in Centers of Power." *Social Science Journal*, 18 (1981), 71–86.

Ishihara, Kunio. "Trends in the Generational Continuity and Succession to Household Directorship." *Journal of Comparative Family Studies*, 12 (1981), 351–63.

Ishino, Iwao. "The *oyabun-kobun*: A Japanese Ritual Kinship Institution." *American Anthropologist*, 55 (1953), 695–707.

Jorden, Eleanor. *Beginning Japanese: Parts One and Two*. New Haven: Yale University Press, 1963.

Kaji, Etsuko. "The Invisible Proletariat: Working Women in Japan." *Social Praxis*, 1 (1973), 375–88.

Kanter, Rosabeth Moss. *Men and Women of the Corporation*. New York: Basic Books, 1977.

Kawashima, Takeyoshi. *Nihon shakai no kazokuteki koosei*. Tokyo: Gakusei Shoboo, 1948.

Kemnitzer, David S. "Sexuality as a Social Form: Performance and Anxiety in America." In *Symbolic Anthropology: A Reader in the Study of Symbols and Meanings*, edited by Janet L. Dolgin, David S. Kemnizer, and David M. Schneider, 292–307. New York: Columbia University Press, 1977.

Kikuchi, Dairoku. *Japanese Education*. London: John Murray, 1909.

Kingston, Maxine Hong. *The Woman Warrior: Memoirs of a Girlhood among Ghosts*. New York: Knopf, 1976.

Kitaoji, Hironobu. "The Structure of the Japanese Family." *American Anthropologist*, 73 (1971), 1036–51.

Kondo, Dorinne. "Dissolution and Reconstitution of Self: Implications for Anthropological Epistemology." *Cultural Anthropology*, 1 (February 1986), 74–88.

———. "Work, Family, and the Self: A Cultural Analysis of Japanese Family Enterprise." Ph.D. diss., Department of Anthropology, Harvard University, 1982.

Koyama, Takashi. *The Changing Social Position of Women in Japan*. Geneva: Unesco, 1961.

———. "Local Variations of Household Forms and Family Consciousness." *Journal of Comparative Family Studies*, 12 (1981), 305–15.

179

———. "The Pre-Modern Peasant Family and Its Life Cycle Pattern." *Journal of Family History*, 8 (1983), 85–108.

Kumagai, Fumie. "Changing Divorce in Japan." *Journal of Family History*, 8 (1983), 85–108.

Kumagai, Hisa A. "A Dissection of Intimacy: A Study of 'Bipolar Posturing' in Japanese Social Interaction—*amaeru* and *amayakasu*, Indulgence and Deference." *Culture, Medicine, and Psychiatry*, 5 (1981), 249–72.

Lebra, Takie Sugiyama. *Japanese Women: Constraint and Fulfillment*. Honolulu: University of Hawaii Press, 1984.

Lévi-Strauss, Claude. *The Elementary Structures of Kinship*. Translated by J. H. Bell, J. R. von Sturmer, and R. Needham. Boston: Beacon Press, 1969.

———. "The Story of Asdiwal." In *The Structural Study of Myth*, edited by Edmund Leach, 1–47. London: Tavistock, 1967.

Lomnitz, Larissa Adler, and Marisol Perez Lizaur. "The History of a Mexican Urban Family." *Journal of Family Histories*, 3 (1978), 392–409.

Marcus, George E. "The Fiduciary Role in American Family Dynasties and Their Institutional Legacy: From the Law of Trusts to Trust in the Establishment." In *Elites: Ethnographic Issues*, edited by George E. Marcus, 221–56. Albuquerque: University of New Mexico Press, 1983.

———. "Spending: The Hunts, Silver, and Dynastic Families in America." *Archives Europeenes de Sociologie*, 26 (1985) 224–59.

Marcuse, Herbert. *Eros and Civilization*. New York: Beacon Press, 1955.

Martin, Samuel E. "Speech Levels in Japan and Korea." In *Language in Culture and Society*, edited by Dell Hymes, 407–15. New York: Harper and Row, 1964.

Matsumoto, Y. Scott. "Notes on Primogeniture in Postwar Japan." In *Japanese Culture: Its Development and Characteristics*, edited by Robert J. Smith and Richard K. Beardsley, 55–69. Chicago: Aldine, 1962.

McClellan, Edwin. Woman in the Crested Kimono: The Life of Shibue Io and Her Family Drawn from Mori Oogai's 'Shibue Chuusai.' New Haven: Yale University Press, 1985.

McLendon, James. "The Office: Way Station or Blind Alley?" In *Work and Lifecourse in Japan*, edited by David W. Plath, 156–82. Albany: State University of New York Press, 1983.

Mills, C. Wright. *The Power Elite*. New York: Oxford University Press, 1956.

Miyashita, Michiko. "Nooson ni okeru kazoku to kon-in." In *Nihon josei shi, III: Kinsei*, 31–62. Tokyo: Tookyoo Daigaku Shuppankai, 1982.

Mochizuki, Takashi. "Changing Pattern of Mate Selection." *Journal of Comparative Family Studies*, 12 (1981), 317–28.

Morioka, Kiyomi. "Family and Housing over the Life Cycle." *Journal of Comparative Family Studies*, 12 (1981), 365–96.

———. "Introduction: The Development of Family Sociology in Japan." *Journal of Comparative Family Studies*, 12 (1981) i–xiii.

Morsbach, Helmut. "Aspects of Nonverbal Communication in Japan." *Journal of Nervous and Mental Disease*, 157 (1973), 262–77.

———. "The Psychological Importance of Ritualized Gift Exchange in Modern Japan." In *Annals New York Academy of Sciences: Anthropology and the Climate of Opinion,* 98–113. New York: New York Academy of Sciences, 1977.

Murakami, Yasusuke, Shumpei Kumon, and Seizaburoo Satoo. *Bunmei to shite no ie shakai.* Tokyo: Chuookooronsha, 1979.

Najita, Tetsuo, and J. Victor Koschmann, eds. *Conflict in Modern Japanese History: The Neglected Tradition.* Princeton: Princeton University Press, 1982.

Nakajima, Bun. *Japanese Etiquette.* Tokyo: Toppan, 1957.

Nakane, Chie. "An Interpretation of the Size and Structure of the Household in Japan over Three Centuries." In *Household and Family in Past Time,* edited by Peter Laslett, 517–43. Cambridge: Cambridge University Press, 1972.

————. *Japanese Society.* Rev. ed. New York: Pelican Books, 1973.

————. *Kinship and Economic Organization in Rural Japan.* New York: Humanities Press, 1967.

Napier, Ron. "The Transformation of the Japanese Labor Market, 1894–1937." In *Conflict in Modern Japanese History: The Neglected Tradition,* edited by T. Najita and J. V. Koschmann, 342–65. Princeton: Princeton University Press, 1982.

Naramoto, Tatsuya, ed. *Zusetsu nihon shomin shi VII: Meiji jidai.* Tokyo: Kawade Shoboo Shinsha, 1962.

Nelson, Donna. "Descent Systems, Affines, and Kindreds: A Rejoinder to Befu." *American Anthropologist,* 67 (1965), 91–95.

Nihon Fujin Dantai Rengoo Kai. *Fujin hakusho 1985.* Tokyo: Harupu Shuppan, 1985.

Norbeck, Edward, and Harumi Befu. "Informal Fictive Kinship in Japan." *American Anthropologist,* 60 (1958), 102–12.

Ohnuki-Tierney, Emiko. *Illness and Culture in Contemporary Japan.* Cambridge: Cambridge University Press, 1984.

Okimoto, Daniel I. *American in Disguise.* New York: Weatherhill, 1971.

Ooguchi, Yuujiro. "Kinsei kooki ni okeru nooson kazoku no keitai: Josei soozokujin o chuushin ni." In *Nihon josei shi, III: Kinsei,* 153–226. Tokyo: Tookyoo Daigaku Shuppankai, 1982.

Ooms, Herman. "The Religion of the Household: A Case Study of Ancestor Worship in Japan." *Contemporary Religions in Japan,* 8 (1967), 201–333.

————. "A Structural Analysis of Japanese Ancestral Rites and Beliefs." In *Ancestors,* edited by William H. Newell, 61–90. Chicago: Aldine, 1976.

Ootake, Hideo. *Ie to josei no rekishi.* Tokyo: Koobundoo, 1977.

Ortner, Sherry B., and Harriet Whitehead. "Introduction: Accounting for Sexual Meanings." In *Sexual Meanings: The Cultural Construction of Gender and Sexuality,* edited by Sherry B. Ortner and Harriet Whitehead, 1–27. Cambridge: Cambridge University Press, 1981.

Osako, Masako Murakami. "Dilemmas of Japanese Professional Women." *Social Problems,* 26 (1978), 15–25.

Ostrander, Susan A. "Upper-Class Women: Class Consciousness as Conduct and Meaning." In *Power Structure Research,* edited by G. William Domhoff, 73–96. Beverly Hills, Calif.: Sage Publications, 1980.

————. *Women of the Upper Class.* Philadelphia: Temple University Press, 1984.

Papanek, Hanna. "Family Status Production: The 'Work' and 'Non-Work' of Women." *Signs: Journal of Women in Culture and Society,* 4 (1979), 775–81.

Pelzel, John C. "Japanese Kinship: A Comparison." In *Family and Kinship in Chinese Society*, edited by Maurice Freedman, 227–48. Stanford: Stanford University Press, 1970.

———. "The Small Industrialist in Japan." In *Explorations in Entrepreneurial History*, edited by Aitken, 79–93. Cambridge: Harvard University Press, 1965.

Plath, David W. *Long Engagements: Maturity in Modern Japan*. Stanford: Stanford University Press, 1980.

———. "Where the Family of God Is the Family: The Role of the Dead in Japanese Households." *American Anthropologist*, 66 (1964), 300–317.

Rabinow, Paul. *Reflections on Fieldwork in Morocco*. Berkeley: University of California Press, 1977.

Radcliffe-Brown, A. R., and Daryl Forde. *African Systems of Kinship and Marriage*. London: Oxford University Press, 1950.

Reinharz, Shulamit. *On Becoming a Social Scientist*. San Francisco: Jossey-Bass, 1979.

Reynolds, David K. *The Quiet Therapies: Japanese Pathways to Personal Growth*. Honolulu: University of Hawaii Press, 1980.

Rohlen, Thomas P. *For Harmony and Strength: Japanese White-Collar Organization in Anthropological Perspective*. Berkeley: University of California Press, 1974.

———. *Japan's High Schools*. Berkeley: University of California Press, 1983.

Rosaldo, Michelle Zimbalist. "Toward an Anthropology of Self and Feeling." In *Culture Theory: Essays on Mind, Self, and Emotion*, edited by Richard A. Shweder and Robert A. LeVine, 137–57. Cambridge: Cambridge University Press, 1984.

———. "The Use and Abuse of Anthropology: Reflections on Feminism and Cross-Cultural Understanding." *Signs: Journal of Women in Culture and Society*, 5 (1980), 389–417.

———. "Women, Culture, and Society: A Theoretical Overview." In *Woman, Culture, and Society*, edited by Michelle Zimbalist Rosaldo and Louise Lamphere, 17–42. Stanford: Stanford University Press, 1974.

Rubin, Gayle. "The Traffic in Women: Notes on the 'Political Economy' of Sex." In *Toward an Anthropology of Women*, edited by Rayna R. Reiter, 157–210. New York: Monthly Review Press, 1975.

Sabean, David. *Power in the Blood: Popular Culture and Village Discourse in Early Modern Germany*. Cambridge: Cambridge University Press, 1984.

Satoo, Tomoyasu. *Keibatsu*. Tokyo: Rippuu Shoboo, 1981.

Schapiro, Meyer. "Style." In *Anthropology Today*, edited by A. L. Kroeber, 287–312. Chicago: University of Chicago Press, 1953.

Schneider, David M. "Kinship, Nationality, and Religion in American Culture: Toward a Definition of Kinship." In *Symbolic Anthropology: A Reader in the Study of Symbols and Meanings*, edited by Janet L. Dolgin, David S. Kemnitzer, and David M. Schneider, 63–71. New York: Columbia University Press, 1977.

———. "What Is Kinship All About?" In *Kinship Studies in the Morgan Centennial Year*, edited by Priscilla Reining, 32–63. Washington, D.C.: Anthropological Society of Washington, 1972.

Sievers, Sharon. *Flowers in Salt: The Beginnings of the Feminist Consciousness in*

Japan. Stanford: Stanford University Press, 1983.

Smith, Dorothy. "Women, the Family, and Corporate Capitalism." *Berkeley Journal of Sociology,* 20 (1975), 55–90.

Smith, Henry Dewitt, II. *Japan's First Student Radicals.* Cambridge: Harvard University Press, 1972.

Smith, Robert J. *Ancestor Worship in Contemporary Japan.* Stanford: Stanford University Press, 1974.

———. "The Domestic Cycle in Selected Commoner Families in Urban Japan: 1757–1858." *Journal of Family History,* 3 (1978), 219–35.

———. "Making Village Women into 'Good Wives and Wise Mothers' in Pre-war Japan." *Journal of Family History,* 8 (1983), 70–84.

———. "Small Families, Small Households, and Residential Instability: Town and City in 'Pre-Modern' Japan." *Household and Family in Past Time,* edited by Peter Laslett, 429–71. Cambridge: Cambridge University Press, 1972.

Smith, Robert J., and Ella Lury Wiswell. *The Women of Suye Mura.* Chicago: University of Chicago Press, 1982.

Soorifu Koohooshitsu. *Seron choosa,* no. 16, October 1984.

Steiner, Kurt. "The Revision of the Civil Code of Japan: Provisions Affecting the Family." *Far Eastern Quarterly,* 9 (1950), 169–84.

Steven, Rob. *Classes in Contemporary Japan.* Cambridge: Cambridge University Press, 1983.

Suenari, Michio. "First Child Inheritance in Japan." *Ethnology,* 11 (1972), 122–26.

Suzuki, Takao. "Language and Behavior in Japan: The Conceptualization of Personal Relations." *Japan Quarterly,* 23 (1976), 255–66.

Swidler, Ann. "Love and Adulthood in American Culture." In *Themes of Work and Love in Adulthood,* edited by Neil J. Smelser and Erik H. Erikson, 120–50. Cambridge: Harvard University Press, 1980.

Tahara, Sooichiroo. *Nihon no pawaa eriito.* Tokyo: Koobunsha, 1980.

Thompson, James D. *Organizations in Action.* New York: McGraw-Hill, 1967.

Tickameyer, Ann R. "Wealth and Power: A Comparison of Men and Women in the Property Elite." *Social Forces,* 60 (1981), 463–81.

Tookyoo Gakugei Daigaku Nihon Shi Kenkyuu Shitsu. *Nihon shi nempyoo.* Tokyo, Tookyoodoo Shuppan, 1984.

Tsubouchi, Yoshihiro, and Reiko Tsubouchi. *Rikon: Hikaku shakaigakuteki kenkyuu.* Tokyo: Soonbusha, 1970.

Tsurumi, E. Patricia. "Female Textile Workers and the Failure of Early Trade Unionism in Japan." *History Workshop Journal,* 18 (1984) 3–27.

Ueno, Kazuo. "Daikazoku, kokazoku, chokkeikazoku: Nihon no kazoku kenkyuu no mittsu no keifu." *Shakaijinruigaku nenpoo,* 10 (1984), 29–50.

Useem, Michael. "Corporations and the Corporate Elite." *Annual Review of Sociology,* 6 (1980), 41–77.

Varenne, Herve. *Americans Together: Structured Diversity in a Midwestern Town.* New York: Teachers College Press, 1977.

Vogel, Ezra F. "The Go-Between in a Developing Society: The Case of the Japanese Marriage Arranger." *Human Organization,* 20 (Fall 1961), 112–20.

———. *Japan as Number One: Lessons for America.* Cambridge: Harvard University Press, 1979.

———. *Japan's New Middle Class.* 2d ed. Berkeley: University of California Press, 1971.

Vogel, Suzanne. "Professional Housewife: The Career of Urban Middle Class Japanese Women." *Japan Interpreter,* 12 (1978), 16–43.

Watanabe, Yoozoo. "The Family and the Law." In *Law in Japan: The Legal Order in a Changing Society,* edited by Arthur Taylor von Mehren, 364–98. Cambridge: Harvard University Press, 1963.

Wax, Rosalie. *Fieldwork: Warnings and Advice.* Chicago: University of Chicago Press, 1971.

Weber, Max. "Bureaucracy." In *From Max Weber: Essays in Sociology,* edited and translated by H. H. Gerth and C. Wright Mills, 196–244. New York: Oxford University Press, 1974.

———. "The Social Psychology of World Religions." In *From Max Weber: Essays in Sociology,* edited and translated by H. H. Gerth and C. Wright Mills, 267–301. New York: Oxford University Press, 1974.

Wolf, Margery. *Women and the Family in Rural Taiwan.* Stanford: Stanford University Press, 1972.

Yanagida, Kunio. *Japanese Manners and Customs in the Meiji Era.* Translated by Charles S. Terry. Tokyo: Oobunsha, 1957.

Yanagisako, Sylvia Junko. "Family and Household: The Analysis of Domestic Groups." *Annual Review of Anthropology,* 8 (1979), 161–205.

———. "Women-centered Kin Networks in Urban Bilateral Kinship." *American Ethnologist,* 4 (1977), 207–26.

Yoshino, M. Y. *Japan's Managerial System: Tradition and Innovation.* Cambridge: MIT Press, 1968.

Zeitlin, Maurice. "Corporate Ownership and Control: The Large Corporation and the Capitalist Class." *American Journal of Sociology,* 79 (1974), 1073–1119.

Zeitlin, Maurice, Lynda Ann Ewen, and Richard Earl Ratcliff. " 'New Princes' for Old? The Large Corporation and the Capitalist Class in Chile." *American Journal of Sociology,* 80 (1974), 87–123.

Index

Accounting, 111

Adoption, 34, 36, 44, 90, 95; and marriage, 100–101

Adulthood, 16–17; *ichininmae no ningen*, 129; and smoking, 16; and sweets, 16. *See also* Marriage

Aijoo, 118

Ancestors, 4–75; cum-gods (*senzo*), 58, 59, 72, 75, 77–78. *See also* Dead, the; Death; Funeral services

Ancestral tablets, 90, 103, 112, 115, 116

Anniversaries, commemorative, 77–78. *See also* Dead, the; Death

Asakusa, 130

Association of Women in Business, 125

Atotori, 17, 95

Ato tsugu, 43

Authority, 50, 87–116, 161; and verticality, 90

Bachnik, Jane, 40–41, 49, 56, 140, 171–72n

Bankruptcy, 68, 107–8

Befu, Harumi, 18, 20

Behavior, organizational, 98–99

Belief, and disbelief, 82–85

Biological descent, 36, 40, 88; and patrilineal descent, 90, 91

Birth, 36, 51; birthday celebrations, 128–30; control, 122; right of, 45, 67, 69; and ritual, 57. *See also*, Childrearing

Boku, 16, 17

Boku senmu, 110–11

Bordieu, Pierre, 3

Bowing, ritual of, 50, 51

Brown, Keith, 87, 88, 101, 148–49

Buddha, 71; Buddhas (*hotoke*), 59, 77, 78; new (*nii-botoke*), 59, 66, 77

Buddhism, 54–57

Bunke. See Family, branch (*bunke*)

Butsudan, 61, 78, 80, 84, 90, 103; care of, 112

Calligraphy, 13

Champon, 129

Childrearing, 33, 122, 155–60. *See also* Birth; Children

Children, 16, 36, 71, 126, 153; death of, 75; education of, responsibility for, 127; exclusion of, from *obon*, 74. *See also* Birth; Childrearing

Choojo, 41, 42, 118, 131, 154

Cigarette smoking, 16

Class boundaries, 6, 9–10, 12–13, 31

Clothing, 41, 47, 71, 81, 92, 144; silk kimono, wearing of, 9–10

Collectivity: of ancestral spirits, 77; and self-sacrifice, 95

Communication, patterns of, 30

185

Moriuchi, Mrs., 50–51, 60–67, 80–81, 92–95
Moriuchi, Nobuko, 60–65, 67, 80–81, 92, 136–39; and *eriito*, 129; friends of, 117; after Makoto's departure, 149–51
Moriuchi, Tasaburo, 97, 108
Moriuchi, Tetsuo, 96, 97, 100, 106, 108–9
Moriuchi Industrial Design and Construction, 96, 105–10
Moriuchi Industries, 62, 63, 92–111
Moriuchi Properties, 97, 106–8
Moriuchi Science and Technology, 62, 63, 97, 105, 149–50
Morsbach, Helmut, 18, 24
Muenbotoke, 70–71; as outsiders, 74–75
Mukaebi, 58, 82–83
Mukoo no nihonjin, 17
Muko-yooshi, 34, 36, 40, 131, 148–51; recruitment of, 43–45, 50, 100; in their new households, 154–55
Muramoto Concern, 151–54
Murdoch, Iris, 92

Naijo no koo, 94
Nakajima, Bun, 13
Nakane, Chie, 6, 48, 87, 90, 131, 170n; on changes in status, 172n; on *shinseki* relationships, 139, 171n
Nakoodo, 124–25, 127–28, 130–35, 32
Names, and status, 68–69
Nari-agari, 5, 137
National Tax Bureau, 110
New Nippon Appliances, 106–7, 109
New Year's celebrations, 103, 112–13
Nii-bon, 64, 69–70; *no kuyoo*, 70
Nii-botoke, 59, 66, 77
Ningen kankei, 94
Ninjoo, 18–24, 46, 50, 140, 161
Nishimura, Mitsuko, 15, 17, 22, 67–68, 111–16, 155–61
Nonaka, Hideo, 136–38
Nookotsu, 65
Nouveau riche, 5
Nyoobo, 121
Nyoobo-yaku, 62

Obasama, 68
Obedience, 109

Objectivity, 83, 84
Obligations, 5, 98, 103, 162; and gift exchange, 18–21, 23, 24; and Japanese social structure, 1–2; and love, 161; surface world of (*tatemae*), 10–11, 17, 134, 135, 143. *See also Giri*
Obon (Festival of the Dead), 55–59, 64, 70–73, 82–83, 103; and the Itoo household, 116; the observance of seasonal rites during, 77
Obon mukai, 55
Ochanomizu University, 15
O-erai-san, 116
Ohaka, 55
Ojoosama, 95, 128
Okaasan, 42
Okimoto, Mr., 28–29, 41–46
Okimoto, Mrs., 28–29, 41–46, 125–27, 130–39, 143–48
Okimoto, Reiko, 41–46, 126, 130–36, 138, 143–45
Okimoto household, 61, 162
Okimoto Paper Products, 147–48
Okinawa, 60
Okinawan descent, 10
Okiyome, 72
Okubo, Shigehisa, 122–24
Okuribi, 58
Okusama, 28, 41–46 *passim*, 60, 63, 72, 74; and the mourning process, 65–66; use of the term, 69
Omekakesan, 62
Omiai, 15, 41–45, 55, 118–41, 150. *See also* Marriage
On, 18–24
Oneesan, 17
Oniisama, 69
Ooms, Herman, 59, 64, 69–70, 72, 75, 82–83
Ore, 16
Osaka, 49
Otaku, 46–51
Otooba, 71, 168n
Otoosan, 42
Oyagaisha, 62, 96
Oyakei, 116
Oyakookoo, 118
Oyome-san (bride), 35, 43–45, 95, 126, 130–36; life of, difficulty of, 143–46, 151, 154–55

Library of Congress Cataloging-in-Publication Data

Hamabata, Matthews Masayuki.
    Crested kimono / Matthews Masayuki Hamabata.
      p. cm.
    Includes bibliographical references.
    ISBN 0-8014-2333-3 (alk. paper)
    1. Family—Japan—Case studies.   2. Family-owned business
enterprises—Japan—Case studies. I. Title.
HO682.H25   1990
306.85'0952—dc20   89-46173